Young Love

An Adoptee's Memoir

Bonnie Parsons

Bonnie Parsons

DESIGNED BY:
Ellie Woznica

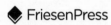

FriesenPress

Suite 300 - 990 Fort St
Victoria, BC, V8V 3K2
Canada

www.friesenpress.com

ISBN
978-1-5255-5129-1 (Hardcover)
978-1-5255-5130-7 (Paperback)
978-1-5255-5131-4 (eBook)

1. FAMILY & RELATIONSHIPS, ADOPTION & FOSTERING

Distributed to the trade by The Ingram Book Company

TABLE OF CONTENTS

NAMES AND TERMS

Names in adoption stories are often confusing. The parents who raised me are my mom and dad, and those names refer only to them.

I have used the terms "birthmother" and "birthfather" since I began searching in the 1980s. Other terms are also used today, but in the interest of clarity and consistency, I use birthmother and birthfather in my memoir.

With a few exceptions for privacy, names have not been changed.

DEDICATION

Identity is sacred.

This memoir is dedicated to

all searchers and search angels.

Never give up!

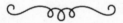

INTRODUCTION

When I was a little girl, my parents often talked about adoption. For me, adoption marked the beginning of my life and my identity. This is not to say we didn't celebrate the day I was born. I loved my birthday, as all kids do. Mom would wrap nickels in wax paper and hide a few of them in the cake. Such excitement! A few years later, I remember requesting chocolate pudding with raisins for dessert on my birthday. But during my childhood, I never thought about the circumstances of my birth, nor the time before my parents came for me at Ville Marie Social Service Centre in Montreal when I was almost eight months old.

I have fond memories of our after-dinner chats. Mom, my brother and sister, and I would linger at the dining room table. Dad had retreated to the living room to finish reading the newspaper while Mom told the three of us family stories--and patiently answered all our questions.

She told me that my birthmother and birthfather were not married. He was a lawyer, and she was his secretary. They were from Montreal, and I was born in Montreal. Because they were not married, they could not keep me. As a child, I heard this as a simple matter of logic and pure common sense. I was adopted because they were not married.

Later, I learned that I had been placed in foster care until my parents picked me up and took me home. My foster mother handed me over to them at Ville Marie. Dad claimed that she seemed old to him. Then he laughed, because she was probably younger than he was now. I asked about any information they were given. Dad smiled and said that he and Mom were thinking only of their new baby girl.

I always knew I was adopted. The beauty of this statement is that I owned it. It belonged to me. My birthfather was a lawyer, my birthmother was his secretary, they could not keep me because they were not married, and so I was adopted by my parents who love me. That was my story. When I shared it, I felt satisfied and safe in my own little world.

Mom understood the value of age-appropriate information. To this day, I love my memories of the after-dinner chats. I was curious and captivated by every detail, no matter how many times I heard them. When each chat ended, I was a happy girl!

My story provided the love and identity I needed. I've told it often to folks who are unfamiliar with adoption and ask questions, like "When did you find out you were adopted?" or "Are your parents your real parents?" I thank my mom for explaining things to me as a youngster and giving me the story that I held onto tightly for so many years. I hear many adoptees say, "I always knew I was adopted." They feel they have always known because they were told at such a young age--a wise strategy for adoptive parents, in my opinion.

My parents were not given any identifying information about my birth families or my birth. My records were sealed forever by law in the Province of Quebec. As a result, as much as I knew someone else gave birth to me, my heart and soul belonged to my parents and my family. There was nothing else to know because the laws restricted any release of identifying information.

~

As I left childhood behind, curiosity about my birthparents seeped into my conscience. I felt frustrated for the first time—*Why doesn't my story start at the beginning?* But I also felt that, perhaps, I should be fine without the whole story. Maybe I didn't need to know everything. Maybe curiosity is overrated. I shuddered at the thought of hurting my parents by even asking for the name of the adoption agency. After all, they had provided me with love and a secure home.

Worry and frustration are very personal feelings experienced by many adoptees. We worry about disappointing loved ones. Dad drove me to piano lessons at night in Sainte-Anne-de-Bellevue in the bitter cold and was concerned about keeping my hands warm before my lesson. Mom and I had tea after school and shared a deep bond of love and trust. How could I not believe that searching for my birthparents would upset them? However, we are often frustrated by sealed records that, if they could only be opened, would unveil identifying information and lead us to birth families, medical histories, and our heritage.

Regulations and procedures for obtaining non-identifying information and identifying information vary greatly from province to province and state to state. Confidentialities are protected by law.

Not surprisingly, curiosity grew from my frustration. Curiosity is a powerful state of mind. As the old proverb goes, *Curiosity killed the cat; satisfaction brought him back!* When curiosity hits me, I'm all in! I cannot ignore it. Curiosity became a driving force in my search for my birthparents and my heritage.

At first, I focused on my birthmother. She had given birth to me. In my late teens, I wanted to know everything about her. While studying for exams during my freshman year of college, I easily distracted myself—daydreaming about our similarities and differences. Over time, I developed the same curiosity about my birthfather.

When I was ready to begin my search, I wanted to talk to my parents without hurting anyone's feelings or causing distress. I did not need another mother or father. I did not need another family. I simply wanted to know who gave birth to me. I wanted to see people who looked like me. I wanted them to know about me, to know that I was doing well. Finally, I wanted to know my heritage, my original identity, which belongs only to me.

Most folks I know have parents who love them, and they have access to their medical histories and ancestry. They do not question their right to know all these things. Nor do they have to defend it. Oftentimes, folks aren't aware that adoptees do not have a right to their original birth certificates and their medical histories.

I started looking for the answers in 1983, thirty-five years ago! Even today, I am aware—and yes, sometimes worried— that people think I am ungrateful. And I'm still frustrated by closed adoption records. Is there a way my worry and frustration surrounding adoption could have been avoided or lessened?

There is a type of adoption chosen now by many families called "open adoption." An excellent definition for open adoption comes from the website *Child Welfare Information Gateway*, entitled: Openness in Adoption, Building Relationships Between Adoptive and Birth Families:

Open adoption is a type of adoption in which birth and adoptive families have some form of initial and/or ongoing contact. Contact may begin with a meeting between an expectant mother and potential adoptive parents. Sometimes, an expectant parent may choose the adoptive family based on such a meeting or other communication. After placement, birthmothers and/or fathers and members of their extended families may interact in various ways with the adoptive parents, as well as with the adopted child or youth. Communication may happen through letters, emails, social media exchanges, telephone calls, or visits. While some families may exchange brief notes and photos, others may spend more time together and celebrate birthdays or holidays together. The type and frequency of contact will be decided by the people involved and can range from several times a month to every few years. Contact often changes as a child ages or as family members' needs and wishes change.

Open adoption, communication between adoptive parents and birthparents, is a huge step up from my closed adoption. There are various forms and levels of communication from which to choose, but I believe even a little is better than none at all.

Most importantly, trust and respect are essential in order to maintain a communication plan that is in the best interest of everyone, especially the child. As the child grows, her story can too. Questions can be addressed and relationships formed. I didn't want another family, but I believe I should have had access to the identity of my birthparents, in the very least when I reached the age of 18.

On her blog, *[birthmother] First Mother Forum*, April 3, 2018, from a piece titled "How adoption narratives encourage eternal separation of mother and child," Lorraine Dusky wrote about open adoptions:

> Today we have a choice to make adoptions be not sealed, not closed. The ethical choice for both birth mothers and adoptive parents is to choose only open adoption, where the natural family, or mother, stays in touch throughout the process. That is the responsibility of both mothers, natural and adoptive. This is not easy for anyone, I suspect, including the child at the heart of every adoption; but if adoption, or legal guardianship, must happen, let it be open from the very first breath. And while I'm imaging a sea-change in attitude, let this all happen without changing the child's birth certificate, but let it reflect the truth of one's birth. Another piece of paper that shows the legal guardianship of a child is not so hard to imagine. It too can come to symbolize love and a lifetime.

~

Most of the adoption professionals in Montreal who helped me with my search were supportive of adoptees and open records. However, they were required to follow the law and deny adoptees, like myself, any identifying information.

In June 2018, the Quebec National Assembly Bill 113, an act to amend the Civil Code and other legislative provisions as regards adoption and the disclosure of information, states:

> An adoptee, including one under 14 years of age who has obtained the prior approval of his father and mother or tutor, has the right to obtain, from the

authorities responsible under the law for disclosing such information, his original surname and given names, those of his parents of origin and information allowing him to contact them. Likewise, once the adoptee has reached full age, his parents of origin have the right to obtain the surname and given name assigned to him and information allowing them to contact him. No such information may be disclosed, however, if an identity disclosure veto or a contact veto, as the case may be, bars their disclosure.

This amendment to the Civil Code is a welcome development for adoptees and families.

~

As I picked up bits and pieces of information during my search for my birthparents, I treated each piece as a valuable clue to finding out who they were. Even the non-identifying information helped me connect the dots! The Quebec laws were not on my side, but my patience and determination, and my family's support gave me the strength to keep searching. Identifying my birthparents would be the key to my original identity and family heritage.

Here is my story.

1

MY FAMILY

My dad was born in 1916 in Ottawa, Ontario, Canada. He was the fifth out of six children. My mom was born in 1920 in Toronto, Ontario, Canada. Mom had one sibling: a younger brother. Tom Brokaw wrote about my parents' generation in his 1998 book *The Greatest Generation*. They lived through the Great Depression and World War II--these men and women valued personal responsibility, duty, honor, and faith.

Even as a child, I recognized that my parents had experienced the tragedies of war and great personal loss, though we were not told many details. They controlled their emotions because that is what their generation did. They chose to move on and did not dwell on the past. However, I have learned that their experiences had a serious and long-lasting impact on their health and well-being.

My parents had strong beliefs and held fast to the social norms of the time. Today, it is well known that discussing difficulties and losses can be life-saving. For my parents, in the mid-20th century, family discussions about difficulties were out of the question—although my mom valued many dear female friendships in her lifetime.

Mom and Dad were both tough. I witnessed time and again situations in which my parents showed courage and held it together more than I could. For example, as an adult, I recall visiting Dad in the hospital and tearing up as Mom and I approached his room. Mom noticed and glared at me. "Do not cry in front of your father."

Dad was a captain in the Canadian Army during WWII. As a scientist with a Ph.D. in biochemistry, he was assigned by the army to do experimental, scientific work. He never described it to us. In fact, he said he never would, except to say that it was morally wrong.

We understood how conflicted he was, having to serve his country during wartime in an assignment he believed to be immoral. I didn't learn the nature of his work until decades later when a book was written about the WWII Canadian research program.

Dad was shocked to find the book while browsing through a book bin in a Kmart store (bargain deals!). It was called *Deadly Allies: Canada's Secret War. 1937-1947 Developing Chemical and Biological Weapons, Including Anthrax, at Suffield, Grosse Isle and Queen's University in Kingston*, written by John Bryden in 1989.

Not surprisingly, we still did not hear details of Dad's wartime assignment even after he found Bryden's book. We knew very little, with only a couple of exceptions. When we were very young, we learned that Dad had spent time in Mexico with the army. While on assignment there, he was exposed to life-threatening bacteria. Mom always told us he had contracted amoebic dysentery. It is also very possible that he became ill from the toxins he was handling. In any case, he became gravely ill and had multiple surgeries, over a period of a number of years, to remove more and more of his large intestine, eventually losing it entirely. Dad's health and well-being would be impacted for his entire life, as were his wife's and children's lives impacted.

Mom grew up in Toronto. In 1940, at the age of 20, she married her high school sweetheart, Fred Curry. Fred was a squadron leader in the permanent Royal Canadian Air Force during WWII. On March 26, 1943, his plane went down in a snowstorm in Alaska. Fred's ashes were scattered on Tamgas Mountain, Annette Island, Alaska.

I was shocked and saddened to find the government documentation of Fred's tragic death online, including the "Circumstances of Casualty":

> Aircraft was on a transportation flight between Ketchikan and Annette Island. Apparently ran into a heavy snow storm, and in attempting to land in Metlakatle Harbour, the aircraft flew into the water, striking with the starboard float or wing first, cartwheeling on the starboard wing, and came to rest on its nose in approximately ten to twelve feet of water. (Position coordinates included.)

Dad left a small note on the kitchen counter at the time of Mom's death in June 2000. Note: *When Mary married Fred, she was 20, had always known him. He joined the Permanent RCAF in the late 1930s, and was lost over the Pacific in 1943.*

Mom told us about her first husband during an after-dinner chat. I recall asking if they had any children. They did not. We had one item in our home that belonged to my mother and Fred: a fine flatware chest. We used it every day.

My mom's parents were our "Nana" and "Grandpa."

Grandpa was a real gentleman, one of the finest and kindest people I have ever known. When Fred died, he told my grieving mother, "It is not as important what happens to you in life as what you do about it." Mom told us how this advice from her father helped her through her grief. My own children have heard me repeat this powerful message over the years.

~

When Dad returned from Mexico, he had no idea how his illness would worsen over time. He and Mom first met on a train somewhere between Toronto and Ottawa. It was the beginning of their loving relationship and marriage of fifty-five years.

The wedding took place June 24, 1944 at Mom's parents' home in Ottawa. Relatives from both families were there, including Dad's mother and brothers and sisters. Dad's father had died in 1935 when Dad was 19.

Recently, I found my parents' engagement announcement and wedding announcement in newspapers.com. Mom was 24 and Dad was 28.

Nana noted key events in her diary:

Monday, May 22, 1944   *Mary bought her wedding dress at the Olive Shop.*

Thursday, June 15, 1944   *Luncheon for Mary at Chateau Laurier*

Saturday, June 24, 1944   *Mary and Don married— quiet wedding. Will live in Kingston, beginning July 2, 1944.*

MOM AND DAD'S WEDDING – JUNE 24, 1944

My mother's brother, George, was five years younger than my mother. He was a leading aircraftman in the Canadian Air Force during the war. Two months after Mom and Dad were married, George was killed in a flight-training accident near Lindsay, Ontario. He was 20 years old. I found his obituary from the *Ottawa Journal*, August 22, 1944. Mom did not often talk about losing her brother. She and George were very close, and as the older sister, she had always been very protective of him. I believe his death was an unspeakable loss for my mother.

Mom said her parents were never the same after George's death. I recall one time in my grandparents' living room in Ottawa. There was a brief discussion about Uncle George. I noticed my grandfather had tears in his eyes. Either my mom

5

or grandmother quickly changed the subject. I was heartbroken to see my grandfather, the finest and kindest gentleman, suffer a father's grief over the loss of a son—his only son.

In the space of a year and a half, Mom lost her first husband and her only sibling to aircraft tragedies. Millions of people suffered similar losses. Whether or not these losses were shared with younger generations over the years, the grief and the memories would linger forever.

~

As noted in Nana's diary, my parents lived in Kingston, Ontario when they were first married. Dad was stationed there with the army. He was an alumnus of Queens University in Kingston, where he'd received his Bachelor of Science degree approximately six year earlier.

They loved to talk about their tiny second-floor apartment and their new life together in Kingston. My brother, Ian George, was born in November 1945. There were stories about getting baby Ian and the stroller up and down the stairs! Years later, in retirement, my parents returned to Kingston. It would be their last big move.

When the war ended, they moved from Kingston to Baie-D'Urfé in the West Island area of Greater Montreal. Dad was on the faculty of McGill University at the Macdonald College campus in Sainte-Anne-de-Bellevue.

His office was upstairs in the Institute of Parasitology. Why on earth would I remember that it was on the second floor? Both of my parents were smokers. One day, Dad and a colleague were carrying a new centrifuge upstairs to their department. Unfortunately, Dad had matches in his pocket, and as they were slowly maneuvering the centrifuge up the staircase, Dad's matches ignited and gave him a nasty burn on his thigh. Children don't forget these things!

At this time, as a young professor, Dad began the fight of his life against the dysentery he'd contracted in Mexico. During his illness, he would be hospitalized at veterans hospitals in Ottawa, Toronto, and Montreal.

Grandpa and Nana helped care for Ian while Mom stayed by Dad's bedside day after day, month after month. He was hospitalized for many months, more than once.

We visited the hospital one time that I recall in the mid-1950s. Dad gave us gifts he made in occupational therapy. Ian's was a leather belt. I recall he made moccasins for my sister and me.

Between hospital stays, Dad returned home to family and work responsibilities. He was a determined young man and always motivated to move forward. Tragically, the surgeries took their toll. He had suffered serious irreversible abdominal nerve damage. As a result, my parents were told they would no longer be able to conceive children.

I recall my mother sharing this information with me when I was about ten. They received the difficult and life-changing prognosis when she was still in her twenties and Dad was in his early thirties.

One of Dad's doctors told Mom to expect that he might be physically abusive with her, due to his disability—I am sure that never happened. However, I have no way of knowing how his illness affected his personality. Perhaps he was the same serious scientist and academician prior to his devastating, though life-saving, surgeries.

Unfortunately, the father I knew was often irritable and unhappy. He was also not well much of the time. Mom kept him alive, quite literally. She took care of him, assisting when he needed her help with the colostomy bag, and later, the ileostomy bag. The family expression was, "Dad's making himself better."

Our family routines revolved around Dad's need for peace and quiet. When things were going well, he was less irritable, but generally unhappy. He gave his best to his scientific work, students, and colleagues. We knew that. I genuinely felt great pride for his extraordinary career. He truly loved his work.

~

Dad was raised in a culture that believed "children should be seen, not heard." Indulging or spoiling children was thought to be terribly wrong and damaging to their development. In addition, during the 1950s, it was not uncommon for parents to believe in slapping and spanking children. *It's for their own good, to teach them a lesson. How else will they learn?*

I doubt my mother was spanked as a child. My grandparents were strict, but I have a feeling their tone or a scowl at Mom or George was sufficient to bring them into line.

Dad's upbringing probably included physical punishment. I say that because he believed it was a necessary part of proper child rearing. However, when paired with his unhappy disposition, our punishments were unnecessarily harsh, in my opinion.

At a very young age, I learned to fear him. In his presence, I was often intimidated. This is not to deny my love for my father. I loved him dearly, but I was afraid of him and often disliked him at the same time.

Once, as a senior in high school, when we discussed my college plans, I felt tears welling up, and he said, "Can't I ever talk to you without you crying?" A serious discussion with my father was intimidating. Over the years, I clearly recall thinking that I would be a different kind of parent with my own children.

However intimidating he could be, Dad was generous and thoughtful. I felt his devotion to all of us. Thanks to Mom's care, he survived his health challenges and lived to the age of 85.

~

When my brother Ian was a toddler, Mom and Dad wanted another child. They decided to adopt. There were more babies available for adoption at that time than there are today. Single women who became pregnant had fewer options. Pregnancy brought great shame to their families. Thus, it was very difficult for a young woman to keep her baby. Women were *strongly* encouraged to give up their babies for adoption. This social prejudice continued in our society for many years.

The province of Quebec had very rigid laws. All forms of birth control and abortion were forbidden. Religion and government were intertwined and very restrictive. It is not surprising that there were babies available for adoption.

I was born at Catherine Booth Hospital in Montreal on April 7, 1949. At that time, there wasn't an urgency for adoptive parents to pick up the baby at the hospital and bond with it as soon as possible. Nor was there empathy for the birthmother and her infant.

My birthmother was required to care for me for my first six weeks. I was then placed in foster care. My parents took me home on December 1, 1949. The following week, I turned eight months old.

~

There is one more *very* important after-dinner chat to recall. My parents had taken me into Montreal for my final evaluation at the adoption agency. The agency was pleased with my growth and development.

Not long after, my parents received a call from the agency regarding a little girl who had been adopted and returned by a couple who thought a baby would save their marriage. The little girl had also been in a number of foster homes under terribly abusive circumstances. The agency asked my parents if they had ever considered adopting another child. The little girl was four years old.

My parents agreed to a weekend visitation, and another one followed. During the second visitation, we all got chicken pox! My sister, Stephanie, never returned to the agency. Our family was now complete. She became the middle child, and I was still the youngest, now by fifteen months. Whenever Mom told us this story, Stephie and I took great pleasure in teasing Ian. "We were chosen; they were stuck with you!"

2

NANA'S DIARIES

My parents were not overly sentimental. I loved my grand-father's photography slide collection and his stamp books. Sadly, I suspect they were thrown out. But I wouldn't let Nana's diaries get away!

"You really want them?" my mom asked.

Fortunately, it wasn't too late. I've treasured them for over forty years. The diaries cover the late 1930s through 1969.

My father pooh-poohed the diaries as superficial accounts of hair appointments, friends' aches and pains, and the weather! He was right, but he missed all the other descriptions of events, both worldly and close to home. The diaries weave the story of life during and following WWII and its impact on families. Over the years, I've searched Nana's diaries for accounts of family holidays, birthdays, and summer vacations at the cottage. All families have stories to tell. How lucky I am that my nana wrote them down.

My grandparents always said grace at mealtime. I remember this one: *God bless this food to our use, and us in thy service. For Christ's sake, Amen*. Nana's diaries describe all the different ways they helped others, from church involve-ment and fundraising to taking care of neighbors. They regularly drove my dad's mother and Aunt Ellie to visit one of Dad's brothers in long-term care. Nana was always baking and taking cookies, Nanaimo Bars, or butter tarts to friends who were recovering from surgery or grieving the loss of a loved one. I am amazed by the number of baby booties and bonnets Nana knit for hospital nurseries and the afghans she crocheted to be sent overseas during the war.

The most compelling diary entries describe our immediate family events and challenges. In the previous chapter, I wrote about my father's disability after WWII and my parents' subsequent decision to adopt my sister and me. Dad's illness impacted our family for years.

At some point, as I was trying to recall the sequence of events regarding Dad's disability from the mid-1940s to the mid-1950s, I turned to Nana's diaries. Over the years, there are a couple of gaps, but during my dad's illnesses, Nana wrote *every* day.

The circumstances and Nana's accounts of them are the cornerstone of my life as an adoptee in this family. Dad may have disparaged them, but Nana's diaries chronicled the story of his suffering and a family's love. Her entries recorded other events that also caused grave shock and sadness.

My parents were married on June 24, 1944. In mid-August, Nana noted my father's first hospital stay. Five days later, Mom's brother, George, was killed in the flight-training exercise. Nana's account is brief and so sad:

August 19, 1944	*Beautiful day*
	George's accident
August 20, 1944	*One of the longest days I*
	ever endured

August 21, 1944   *George's funeral*
          Poured rain. Cleared
          about 3pm

Nana often reported on world news. She and my grandfather read the *Ottawa Globe and Mail* newspaper and watched news on television. Nana's diary entries expressed not only events, but their worries about world peace and the future. Reading her accounts can take you to that time and place:

In May 1945   *Expecting news any*
          hour that Germany
          has surrendered.

          War over
          VE Day Celebration

~

In November of 1945, everyone welcomed my brother, Ian, who was born in Kingston, Ontario.

The following year, my father was admitted to the Ottawa Veterans' Hospital. I am sure no one thought he would be there very long. Occasionally, Dad was allowed to go home for a day or a holiday weekend. After five months, he was moved to Toronto for surgery. He was finally released after seven and a half months!

Nana's diaries provide dates and a few details. As time went on, she included more medical information. Here are the highlights:

November 21-22, 1946   *Don in hospital.*
          Veterans Wing

November 26, 1946	Don started treatments
December 25, 1946	Don out of hospital for a few hours
December 31, 1946	Don out of hospital for holiday
January 2, 1947	Don back in hospital

The pattern of home visits continued from January 1947 until mid-March. Mom visited Dad once and often twice a day. My grandparents took care of baby Ian.

March 17, 1947	Don moved to private room at hospital.
March 18, 1947	Don had a bad day, treatments, had chills
March 31, 1947	They gave Don a blood transfusion
April 2, 1947	Mary—hospital in evening. Don not feeling well
May 20, 1947	Don moved to Toronto to Christie Street Veterans' Hospital

On June 14, 1947, Dad had his first major operation. His brother, Tom, and my Aunt Kay were there with my mother. Dad was very ill for a couple of days and my grandfather flew from Ottawa to be with my mother. Nana then reported each day that Dad was improving.

June 19, 1947	*Good report from Don*
June 20, 1947	*Don still improving* *Busy looking after Ian*
June 23, 1947	*Mary home—Did not do much, we had so much to talk about re. Don's condition and so many phoned.*
July 4, 1947	*Mary and Harold (Dad's brother) in Toronto*
July 11, 1947	*Don phoned from Oakville that he would be home on Monday.*
July 14, 1947	*Don arrived home after 2 months at Christie Street Hospital in Toronto* *Art (my grandfather) took Mary to meet him at 11pm*

Dad's condition quieted down after his operation, and he regained his strength. He was hired by McGill University, and they purchased a house in Baie-d'Urfé. My grandparents visited from Ottawa frequently. They helped with my brother as well as house and garden chores.

By April 1948, Dad was back in the hospital—this time the Veterans Hospital in Montreal.

April 29, 1948	*Don in hospital*

April 30, 1948	*Don to have operation. Severe operation, more intestines removed than anticipated*
Early May 1948	*Don critically ill.*
May 8, 1948	*Don still very, very ill Art and Mary met with superintendent of hospital Don very ill—all worried*
May 10, 1948	*Don is very thin & stomach won't hold food hiccups and nausea*
May 15, 1948	*Don improved*
May 20, 1948	*Don much better, but still on mostly liquids*
May 21, 1948	*Don's mother and Art in Ste. Annes*
May 27, 1948	*Don improving nicely, gaining weight, spending most of the day in a wheelchair on the hospital sun porch*

June 1948 was a roller coaster of uncertainty. Dad was home and gaining strength, then back in the hospital on June 21st. His brother Bruce visited.

June 29, 1948

Don very ill, operation necessary and doctor says his chances are slight.
Then:
Good news, colostomy had started to function so they did not need to operate. Don still very ill.

July 7, 1948

Don's throat and nose very sore from tubes, expecting to operate any day

July 14, 1948

Operation
Don doing as well as could be expected large blood transfusion

Many relatives were by Dad's side.

July 19, Nana wrote,

Don's condition very favorable, had custard.

On July 29, 1948, he came home.

Sadly, Dad was back in the hospital in November. He improved for two weeks, but became very ill again.

November 21, 1948	*Don severe hemorrhage Mary asked Tom to come at once Tom and Kay drove from Ottawa*
November 22, 1948	*Don critically ill*
November 24, 1948	*Don improved, no immediate danger Tom & Kay went home*
November 25, 1948	*ill*
December 14, 1948	*Don becoming discouraged, he is losing ground so they are to operate*
December 15, 1948	*Anxious days— pending Don's operation Friday*
December 16, 1948	*Anxious day*
December 17, 1948	*Don survived surgery appeal for blood, Dr. Miller got donors*
December 18, 1948	*Don very weak, but still alive Doctors marvel at his resistance Mary encouraged*

The family had gathered once again and all were very happy. However, the success of the operation was short-lived. In January 1949, Dad's bladder was not functioning well. He had a high fever, nausea, and diarrhea. They did a tidal irrigation of the bladder and he showed improvement. But then on January twentieth, they operated on his bladder.

On February 6, Dad went home for his birthday weekend after being hospitalized for three months. He was discharged soon after that. Unbelievably, Dad had sinus surgery as well, on May 3, 1949. The operation was successful.

November 24, 1949	*Mary called—going for Bonnie on December 1st*
December 1, 1949	*Don and Mary went to Montreal to get the new baby*

~

For the next eight years, Dad survived without further abdominal surgery. My sister arrived and we were a busy family of five. Mom was Dad's rock—in sickness and in health!

However, in August 1957, something went terribly wrong. Dad was back in the VA hospital in Montreal. Family started arriving and friends took care of the three of us. Dad was on antibiotics and everyone was hoping they would not need to operate. Nana described what happened next.

September 6, 1957

*Home all day waiting
for call from Mary about
Don. It came about one.
Don is very ill after a
major operation. They
found his bowel twisted
for ten feet and twisted
around his stomach. They
could not get his veins for
feeding and Dr. Gardner
had to go back and put
tube in his jugular vein—*

*They have special nurses
on with him. They think
he will make a rapid
recovery as he will soon
be able to take food orally
as there was no internal
cutting and stitching. Dr.
Gardner told Mary he
had never seen anything
to compare with the
condition he found and he
wishes he had operated
sooner. We are concerned
about Don but hope and
pray he can weather
this ordeal for a couple
of days until he can
take nourishment.*

September 7, 1957

Left early for Ste. Annes. Mary was very tired. She had such a hectic day in the hospital yesterday when Don was so very ill—He just about slipped away before they got the intravenous feeding going in his jugular vein. Poor fellow, what an ordeal he has been through. Mary so tired and worried.

Mom told us a couple of remarkable details that I've never forgotten. With his scientific background, Dad understood his illness and conferred with his doctor. In one situation, the doctor disagreed with Dad. As Mom told us, she took the doctor out in the hall and gave him a piece of her mind. The doctor took Dad's advice and the treatment was successful.

Mom told us that Dad was declared dead twice. He was so weakened that they could not find a pulse. She described how each time she had gotten really close to him, whispering softly, and his pulse returned.

I was 8 years old when Dad had surgery in 1957. I remember it was a very scary time. He was home and still very ill and needed a frame over his bed so that the bedding would not touch the boils on his body. I recall the horribly frightening sight. I can't imagine how my parents got through it. Nana reported on October 27, *Don's boils better.*

Dad had one more operation related to his ileostomy. We were living in Amherst, Massachusetts by this time. Nana wrote on February 25, 1967, *Mary took Don to the hospital in Boston*. That is the only reference to the hospitalization. I don't believe Dad's life was in danger. I was away at school. I recall that he had surgery to improve the functioning of the ileostomy and recovery went well. His equipment *to make himself better* was updated and easier to manage.

~

Mom and Dad were fiercely independent and thorough with regard to end-of-life planning. Their *Do Not Resuscitate* (DNR) documents had grids with levels of treatment for different conditions. Dad noted that he did not want any lifesaving intervention if his suffering was related to his ileostomy.

After Mom's death, Dad lived in an assisted-living apartment in Kingston, Ontario. One night, he suddenly became very seriously ill. He signaled for help and was rushed to the hospital. A blood clot had formed in his bowel. Unfortunately, his DNR document was not available and he underwent emergency surgery. We faxed our copy of the DNR to the hospital. After a couple of days, it was recommended that he be taken off life support.

We were by his side until he died peacefully, early on the morning of April 5, 2001. He was 85 years old. At one point near the end, he remarked, "There's Mary, and the others." Dad would have pooh-poohed that, much as he pooh-poohed Nana's diaries.

The spirit of love is pretty powerful, Dad. With Nana's diaries, we have an account of your decades-long, heartwrenching battle to stay alive, and the determination of Mom and the family to be there for you. It's a true love story.

3

HEREDITY OR ENVIRONMENT

My parents were not given my medical history. I came without special instructions or restrictions! All of my records were sealed. I am very grateful for my good health. Mom and Dad never had to request medical information about my birth family before a Montreal judge in order for doctors to treat a life-threatening illness.

Had I been ill, there was no guarantee that a request for my records would be granted. These situations required open-mindedness and compassionate decision-making. The law, on the other hand, did not invite requests that were exceptions to the rule. Sealed records were to remain sealed forever.

~

I am aware of many traits and abilities I inherited from my birthparents, such as eye-hand and fine-motor coordination. I loved playing the piano, sewing, swimming, bike riding, and ice skating. I would challenge anyone to pick-up sticks, jacks, or hopscotch!

There is no way for me to easily separate my favorite activities into inherited abilities on the one hand or environmental factors on the other. For example, my love for pick-up sticks—I really enjoyed the challenge of removing sticks without disturbing the others. I recall practicing alone when I was about 5 years old, in preparation for the next match. It still makes me smile.

I ice skated in the winter as often as I could. We lived down the street from the outdoor rink behind our church on Maple Avenue—across the street from our school! I remember practicing my skating skills for a Girl Guides badge. There might have been an adult in the little hut beside the rink, but there was *no* supervision--the freedom made it so much fun! We formed two lines across the rink and charged at each other in a game we called "posse."

The little hut had a couple of benches and a pot-belly stove. I tried to dry my icy, snowy mittens, but I just managed to melt the ice and snow--I then had very wet, but warm mittens. But, I didn't care. Hanging out with friends at our rink, when it was getting dark in the late afternoon, left me with the fondest memories!

Many inherited physical traits are nurtured by one's environment. Those who can sing in tune may be encouraged to pursue music. Children, especially adopted children, actually guide parents with their enthusiasm for activities such as music and sports. I loved playing the piano. I took lessons, not only because I begged to but because my parents could afford them and supported my interest.

My dad called me "Little Miss I know who I am and I know where I'm going." We are all born with predispositions or inherited tendencies to behave in certain ways. Dad pretty much nailed mine! Adoptees often feel that their traits are quite different from their adoptive parents and siblings. I've read adoptee accounts of being the only quiet one in a loud house or being the loud one in a quiet house. Recently I read an account of a very short gal visiting her birth family for the first time. She was thrilled to be with other short folks, having been raised in a tall family!

In our strictly disciplined home, we had to have permission to come and go to our various activities. Sometimes Dad approved my requests, other times, not so much. Sadly, there never was an attempt to discuss a situation, to hear both sides, and come to an agreement. These conflicts were upsetting to me and I felt a little like an outsider. Our family dynamics were often complicated--perhaps that is true for all families. I had no biological relatives and so my nature verses nurture preferences and abilities are difficult to define.

Dad ruled the roost--not being allowed to go out on a school night was a tough one. Cousin Neil from Watertown was about my age and played the bassoon brilliantly. We were both in eleventh grade. I recall one occasion when he was invited to play with the Boston Symphony Orchestra, substituting for his bassoon instructor who was a member of the distinguished orchestra. I was so proud of him and excited! And it was going to be televised. This was during a stretch of time when we didn't have a TV, so I needed permission to watch it at my friend's place, three houses up the street. "Sorry, it's a school night and you know the rule." It didn't matter that Neil was Dad's nephew.

Well, I locked myself in the downstairs bathroom and sobbed until I couldn't sob anymore. My mother was beside herself, but she couldn't do anything. Dad was upstairs in bed reading—a routine to keep him well. Mom was simply his messenger. And it didn't occur to me to disobey. I loved my father, but there wasn't much to *like* that night. As parents, Paul and I believe that rules are meant to be broken!

~

I have a fearful, nervous side, which is clearly a combination of my predisposition and my environment. I've wondered, however, if it is related to being separated from my birth-mother after six weeks and then being separated from my foster mother before I was 8 months old when she handed me over to my parents. I have no idea. My father was intimidating, as I have described, and I was very afraid of him.

Certain events in my childhood made me shudder with fear. Dad's illness was always extremely scary. When I was in second grade, an ambulance came for Dad. I hid from sight, overcome with fear. The memory still brings tears to my eyes. Another time, I joined Mom in their bedroom after she got home from the hospital. She said quietly, "We almost lost your father tonight." If you had said the world was coming to an end, I would have agreed. At the age of 8, I stood silently in panic and disbelief.

I was afraid of unfriendly, cold surroundings, both indoors and out. I like a warm, safe, and cozy environment. Oddly enough, I didn't like our house on Maple Avenue in Sainte-Anne-de-Bellevue. I didn't like the style nor the stucco. I was six years old when we moved in and our house felt cold to me.

When my parents bought our first TV, Ian, Stephie, and I watched cops and robbers shows before dinner in our second-floor family room. As soon as someone was shot, I left the room and went downstairs. Those scenes felt too real to me. I remember sitting alone in the living room. You can imagine that I'm not a fan of high suspense or horror films today. My favorite shows back then were *Our Miss Brooks*, *Leave It to Beaver*, and *Father Knows Best*—required viewing!

I often woke up in the middle of the night, frightened and shaking. Disturbing my parents was not an option! I'd get up and go into the bathroom. I had a little routine to calm myself down. I stood in front of the mirror and simply looked at my reflection. We carried on a silent conversation. *You look okay. Really, you do. You'll be fine. Everything is okay. Maybe a little smile, maybe not.* When I stopped shaking and felt calm, I returned to my bed. I was a pro at walking quietly on the old hardwood floors. As far as I know, my family slept through my middle-of-the-night pep talks. That was always a relief!

～

We belonged to the Union Church of the United Church of Canada. My official adoption documents came from the church. The Certificate of Judgment, February 3, 1951 states:

> This is to certify that the following is a true copy of a record of an Act of Civil Status taken by me from the Register of Births, Marriages and Deaths, belonging to Union Church in the United Church of Canada ... Judgment has been rendered on the twenty-second day of January 1951 ordering the adoption of Eleanor Mary Fairbairn, born on the seventh day of April 1949.

Dad and the minister, F.A.C. Doxsee, signed it. I was named after Dad's sister, my Aunt Ellie, and my mother, Mary--Bonnie is a nickname. Church and government official responsibilities overlapped in Quebec.

Mom made sure we attended important church events and services. I remember singing in the junior choir. Dad always said that he didn't go to church because he couldn't sing! Wherever we lived, I always felt it was important to join a congregation.

We learn to live with who we are. I knew I was adopted, and I accepted adoption as part of my identity. As I got older, I rarely disclosed it to others, with the exception of medical folks. Friends and neighbors would comment that I looked like our mother and that Stephie looked like Dad.

One day, Dad and I were chatting, and he referred to a trait we shared as being "in the genes." I was taken aback and never forgot that moment in which he just thought of me as his daughter.

Dad was extraordinarily dedicated to his scientific work. His accomplishments in biochemistry and parasitology were recognized locally and around the world by scientists in his field. I was very proud of him. It was easy for me to sing his praises--it went like this: *My dad is brilliant. I think he's a genius ... but, I'm not bragging about myself, because I was adopted!* It worked!

~

I am surprised that so many people are not at all interested in their biological ancestors, even though the information is readily available to them. On the other hand, as an adoptee, I am not allowed access to information about my ancestors, and yet I love family history and genealogy.

My dad's older brother, my Uncle Harold, was the keeper of the Fairbairn family tree as well as fascinating stories passed down from one generation of Fairbairns to another. It wasn't *my* biological family tree, but I truly enjoyed studying Uncle Harold's work and discussing it with family members over the years.

My favorite story was recorded by my father's great-aunt Eliza. Aunt Eliza was born August 10, 1824 in Edinburgh, Scotland. She died January 7, 1909 in Carleton, Ontario, Canada. Aunt Eliza was the sixth of eight children born to Elspeth (Betty) and Thomas (Tom) Fairbairn.

According to Uncle Harold, sometime between 1875 and 1895, Aunt Eliza wrote, *Recollections of Miss Eliza*

Fairbairn. I cherish my copy of Aunt Eliza's 26-page, hand-written memoir. In 1828, Eliza and her family departed from Edinburgh for Montreal, as Eliza said, *"leaving the old country."*

It wasn't long before the ship encountered ice barges. Eliza wrote:

I remember Father coming down from the deck where he had been looking at the ice barges that were all around. His face was as white as a sheet. His hands shook as he came to Mother. "Oh, Betty, Betty, The Captain says there is no hope. The field of ice is the most he has ever seen. The ship must go down."

Father went up again to the deck but soon returned, saying, "Betty, the Captain says he may save the grown-up people by their getting onto a long boat or raft. They are trying to do something about it now. But you and I will go down with the children. What do you say?" "Oh, Tom, we'll not part. We will go together."

With that, the ship gave another lurch, and someone said, "We are sinking."

Eliza went on to describe how her father convinced the ship's captain to have the sailors and men on board each hold a spar and line them up along the side of the ship to break the force of the ice as it approached.

God blessed the effort ... at last we sailed into open sea.

Eliza's father was praised by the captain for saving the ship from disaster.

Peter, my dad's grandfather and Eliza's younger brother, was 2 years old during the voyage. My dad's great-grandfather, Thomas, lead the ship's crew with his ingenious plan and saved many lives that have since given us six generations of Fairbairns! I am reminded of my nana's diaries. All families have joys and sorrows, ups and downs. How fortunate when someone like Aunt Eliza or my nana record events and experiences for future generations.

As a child, I lived peacefully with my adoption story. I understood it. In fact, I was proud to be adopted. However, as a young adult and then as a mom, without information and without the ability to acquire information, I became frustrated—proud, but frustrated. I wanted to have access to what I believed was mine.

I didn't like the fact that the government in Quebec made decisions regarding my right to my identity. Furthermore, Quebec had not updated its archaic laws, even though successful changes had been made to adoption laws in neighboring provinces.

As a young mother, searching for my original identity took root in the back of my mind. I knew that beginning a search meant asking my parents for any information they had. I needed to start my search with my parents!

But first, I need to retrace my steps back to Glenaladale Terrace.

4

I CALLED IT HOME

Glenaladale Terrace on Macdonald College Campus, Sainte-Anne-de-Bellevue, Quebec

In the late 1940s, Mom and Dad moved with Ian from the house in Baie-D'Urfé to Glenaladale Terrace, a row-house rental on the Macdonald College campus. It was my first home after foster care. I have early memories of our four years there.

BONNIE, NEWLY ADOPTED – 8 MONTHS OLD

IAN AND BONNIE – BIG BROTHER ~ LITTLE SISTER

MOM AND BONNIE

For my second birthday, Ian invited all the neighborhood kids to a birthday party. Mom learned about the party when the kids arrived! She loved to tell that story. A group photo helped me remember it! I wonder where that photo is today.

When I was 3 or 4, I clearly recall imagining the goings-on at Mom's bridge parties. I was upstairs and wished I could sneak down. I pictured all the ladies on the living-room rug forming bridges with their bodies and going under each other's bridges—such a funny memory!

Curran's Lake Summer Cottage, Laurentian Mountains, Quebec

In 1952, my parents bought a summer cottage on Curran's Lake, in the Laurentian Mountains, fifty miles northwest of our home in Sainte-Anne-de-Bellevue. We spent summers at the cottage from the time I was 3 until I was 13. We would leave Sainte-Anne-de-Bellevue the first day of summer vacation and return Labor Day weekend.

Ian, Stephie, and I loved the cottage. We were outside all the time, swimming, exploring the woods, and playing with kids from neighboring cottages. We were allowed to go barefoot all the time. I remember knowing each rock and root, twist and turn in our paths through the woods. We ran along and usually did not fall. One day, I stubbed my big toe and never felt it. Later, seeing the blood, I realized what had happened. Sadly, with an injury like this, we were required to wear socks and shoes until it healed.

Dad worked all week and came up to the cottage Friday evenings. I felt sorry for Mom. Dad had our only car and the closest store was a mile away on a gravel road. Mom had few friends up at the cottage. I don't recall that we had a telephone. There might have been mail delivery. I know it was difficult for her. I don't know how she endured it.

Dad brought one of Ian's friends on occasion and relatives visited. Grandpa and Nana spent a couple of weeks with us each summer, which everyone loved. And who could forget the iceman's weekly delivery of blocks of ice for our icebox? All visitors were a welcome treat!

One summer, on a walk in the woods with Ian, our dog, Jack, got in a major fight with a porcupine. Ian stabbed and killed the porcupine with his knife! Ordinarily, the knife he carried in his belt sheath was used for smaller projects like whittling fine tips on marshmallow sticks.

Ian brought Jack home, and he and Dad took him to the vet. Fortunately, Dad and the car were at the cottage! Many quills were extracted. They were in his mouth and everywhere else! For months, we'd feel a quill surfacing in poor Jack's fur and run for the pliers. Jack was a good dog. My parents were very attached to him. I'm sure he was a comfort to Mom at Curran's Lake.

On Fridays, Dad would bring a fresh supply of groceries. Watermelon was a family favorite. We kids would stand on the open deck and see who could spit seeds the farthest.

I was brave and adventurous at the cottage, though fearful on occasion, such as Jack's porcupine fight. Overall, the joys of outdoor freedom and activities that I loved carried the day. I won an underwater swimming race in the Curran's Lake Regatta in the mid-50s! When we were old enough, we each swam across the lake and back, about a half-mile round trip. Dad rowed next to us, offering encouragement along the way.

Dad and Ian loved to fish! They would take the big, old wooden rowboat out in the evening and catch bass. It was not unusual for them to catch a dozen or so in one outing. Dad would clean the fish for breakfast the next morning. He also cooked the fish, though he was the only one who didn't like to eat them. Mom taught us how to peel the filets away from the bones. Fried bass and toast was our favorite weekend breakfast.

I never had an interest in wrapping a worm around a hook. But, at a young age, I was intrigued by the fish-cleaning process and soon became a pro! Dad taught me how to skin the fish, remove the insides, head, and fins, and then clean it up. Perched on a stool in front of the kitchen sink, I took pride in getting my fingers under the skin and carefully removing it without wasting any flesh. After all, this was breakfast!

In retrospect, my funniest memory at Curran's Lake occurred out on the water, when Stephie and I were alone in the big, old wooden rowboat. We got into a fight, as we were known to do. It soon got physical, and we battled each other with the large wooden oars. Eventually, we knocked the oars out of each other's grasp and into the lake. I can still see the oars drifting away from us.

Suddenly the fight was over, and we were in an embrace yelling for help. Dad came out in the canoe and fetched the oars for us. He had stern words and revoked our boating privileges for a while. Stephie and I had a pattern throughout our early childhood of fighting and then banding together as punishment loomed.

9 Maple Avenue, on Macdonald College Campus, Sainte-Anne-de-Bellevue, Quebec

We moved to 9 Maple Avenue before I started kindergarten. Our house was only about fifty yards from Glenaladale Terrace. Our backyard adjoined the backyard of the Terrace. Again, we rented from Macdonald College. I'm sure our parents were thrilled to have more room. We had a short walk to our school, which was on the campus, and we came home for lunch. Even the bus kids were bussed home for lunch

MOM AND DAD, BONNIE, IAN AND STEPHIE -1955

The Macdonald College campus was home to the Department of Education, in addition to Agriculture, Home Economics, and the Institute of Parasitology where Dad worked. Entire education classes from the college routinely sat in the back of our classrooms observing instruction. I remember feeling a little anxious for my teachers.

BONNIE IN GRADE 1

I fell in love with school in kindergarten. In fact, while in kindergarten, I decided I wanted to be a teacher when I grew up—and I did. I was not the best student, but I loved the structure of each day, the activities, and materials. And I loved being with my friends.

Winters were very cold in Sainte-Anne-de-Bellevue. Back then, no one talked about wind chill. We walked to school, all bundled up, when the temperature was minus twenty-five. The scarves over our mouths were frozen stiff by the time we got to school, no more than a quarter mile away.

In first grade, my parents signed me up for ballet lessons. At first, I enjoyed them. My best friend, Fiona, was in the class too. One evening, I demonstrated the ballet positions and a plié for my parents. Ian was there, unfortunately, and rolled on the floor laughing hysterically at my plié. That was it! The next week, instead of going to ballet, Fiona and I hid in her basement. Our frantic parents found us eventually, and we never had to go to ballet again.

EMILY AND RONNIE IN MOM'S GINKGO TREE, AT MACDONALD COLLEGE, SAINTE-ANNE-DE-BELLEVUE – JULY 1988

The Macdonald College campus was a perfect environment for children. We rode our bikes everywhere, even through the underground walkways. We played games and climbed trees.

Mom blew her yellow whistle when it was time for us to come home for lunch or dinner.

I had a very favorite tree, a ginkgo tree, not far from Glenaladale Terrace. I imagined living in it! I would climb up and lay my head on a lovely, smooth knot and pretend to sleep. Years later, during the search for my birthmother, my husband, children, and I visited Sainte-Anne-de-Bellevue on our way to Montreal. I made sure to take photos of our children in my ginkgo tree.

~

As I've discussed, my father's health stabilized somewhat when I was about 9 years old. Years prior, Dad's surgeries to remove portions of his diseased large intestine had left him with a colostomy bag glued to his skin. The management of this process back then was difficult and often tedious and challenging. Mom was called upon frequently to assist.

By 1957, his large intestine had been completely removed, and he had an ileostomy, in which the end of the small intestine, or ileum, is attached to the opening. Complications would follow, but he lived with the ileostomy for the rest of his life.

Dad's improved health brought more peace to the family. As with all families, we had issues, but *life and death* was no longer atop of the list. I think I was becoming a little tougher, too.

~

My brother, Ian, took piano lessons and hated them. He wanted to play the guitar. I was thrilled when Mom and Dad allowed him to switch and let me take piano lessons. The piano was in our large first-floor hallway, and I practiced every day. I'm surprised, as I think about it, that my siblings never complained. Mind you, they were nowhere in sight!

Once in a while, after I finished practicing the assignments from my piano teacher, I'd take out my favorite songbooks and play one piece after another, just for fun. Mom was nearby in the kitchen preparing dinner, and occasionally she'd suggest that perhaps I had played long enough for one day.

In high school, our piano was in a first-floor spare bedroom. Being older and more self-conscious, I always shut the door and hoped no one was listening. Dad would periodically tease and yell "flat" from the living room.

My parents came from musical families. Dad played the clarinet, and Mom took piano for years. I later learned that I came by my interest in music naturally too. I am so fortunate that I was in a supportive, musical family.

~

As I discovered later, my passion for sewing also came naturally. I'm delighted to recall that my mom was my first sewing teacher. She taught me how to knit and embroider and use a sewing machine.

One afternoon at 9 Maple, she inspired my friend, Mary, and me to make skirts using the sewing machine. Mary and I walked to D'Aoust's department store in Sainte-Anne-de-Bellevue and purchased fabric and matching thread. No pattern necessary!

Mom taught us how to measure and gather the fabric for the waist. We made the waistband as wide as we wanted, mine was a good two to three inches wide. We sewed hooks and eyes in place of buttons and buttonholes. Finally, we hemmed our new skirts. I loved that skirt and got a lot of wear out of it. Mine was lavender and Mary's was blue.

Together, Mom and I sewed a couple of things after that skirt, so that I could learn how to use patterns and make more complicated clothes. In particular, we worked hard together on a shirtdress for me. Mom sewed on one sleeve and then I sewed on the other. She sewed half of the collar, and I sewed the other half. That little dress provided me with many key sewing lessons. After that, I was on my own.

I often made my own clothes, including suits and winter coats, my wedding gown, and eventually clothes for my children and my friends' children too. I loved making toys and Christmas decorations. I think I had an inherited inclination, but Mom was clearly my inspiration.

Baltimore, Maryland and Amherst, Massachusetts

In 1959, Johns Hopkins University in Baltimore, Maryland offered Dad a one-year visiting professorship. We left Jack at home with friends and headed south! My parents rented a beautiful center-entrance brick colonial home. The owner took a liking to Dad and lowered her price so that Dad could afford it!

Needless to say, I loved that house! It was fully furnished. There were winter carpets and summer carpets. Each bedroom had its own bathroom. It even had an intercom system! It was in a beautiful neighborhood with back alleys. For some reason, I love back alleys.

Mom threw me a surprise birthday party in the beautiful sunroom! I stayed in contact with my closest Baltimore friend for many years. She came up to Sainte-Anne-de-Bellevue for a week in the summer following our year in Baltimore.

After Dad's sabbatical, we returned to Macdonald College for just two years.

In 1962, Dad accepted a position at the University of Massachusetts in Amherst. This time, Jack came with us! Ian, Stephie, and I skipped and repeated grades with each of these moves. In Quebec, students graduate from high school after eleventh grade. When we moved from Quebec to the United

States, we were placed a grade ahead so that we were the same number of years from graduation as our friends in Quebec. I went from grade four in Quebec to grade six in Baltimore. When we returned, I joined my classmates for sixth and seventh grades.

In Amherst, I was placed in ninth grade. I never attended fifth grade or eighth grade, but I went to sixth grade twice. I was 17 when I graduated from Amherst Regional High School, the same age I would have been at graduation in Quebec. But I wasn't in Quebec!

In my opinion, there was no need to place us with students one year older than we were. However, I made wonderful friends, and I had a fabulous time. I graduated from college in 1970 and started teaching that fall.

Narragansett, Rhode Island

Nineteen seventy was a big year for me. In January, Paul and I got married. I turned 21 in April. In June, we graduated from the University of Massachusetts Amherst. At the end of the summer, Paul and I moved to Narragansett, Rhode Island.

Paul started graduate school, and I started teaching. I was a fifth-grade teacher in Charlestown for four years. I was young and looked even younger. During a field trip to an art museum in Providence, the docent asked, "Who's the teacher here?"

Buffalo, New York

In June 1974, I resigned from Charlestown, and we moved to Western New York. Paul entered the doctoral program in counseling psychology at the State University of New York at Buffalo--UB for short. My mother always said, "Follow your husband." Fortunately, I was happy to move. I love trying new things and exploring new places.

Paul and I had two requirements for our new home in the Buffalo area. First, we needed an apartment that would allow our dog, Pongo. Pongo was half German wirehaired pointer and half standard poodle. He weighed about eighty pounds! Second, we needed to be able to get my piano in the front door by ourselves. This was a DIY, one-car plus a U-Haul truck operation.

We found an apartment in a row house, surprisingly similar to Glenaladale Terrace at Macdonald College, with a living room, dining room, kitchen downstairs, two bedrooms, and a bath upstairs. We entered the garage from a back alley, which I loved! The garage also had storage space and laundry hook-ups.

I got a teaching job in an excellent school district not far from the apartment. I worked in that district for the next thirty-four years—minus two maternity leaves.

During my young adult years, I had not felt the need to search for my birth family. I was healthy, and therefore I didn't need to talk to doctors about being adopted and having no medical history. I was also very busy in my new career. We were waiting for Paul to get his degree and a job before we started a family.

Curiosity about my birthparents lay dormant during this time. But that was about to change. I had experienced feelings of curiosity and frustration over the years. Now as a young mom, it was time to take action!

5

MOTHERHOOD, MY FIRST INQUIRY

Our son, Ron, was born in 1978, and our daughter, Emily, was born in 1980. I always told them that they were gifts from God.

I knew in my heart that my job was to take care of them, to love them, and to prepare them to become independent and contributing members of society. Strange as it may seem, those were the thoughts that ran through my mind as I got them dressed for the day, puréed veggies, and figured out my new role as a mom.

Years before, I had decided to be a different sort of parent than my own parents had been. I read a lot and became a La Leche League mom and leader. La Leche League is a nonprofit organization that offers education and support related to breastfeeding and parenting, in general. I cherished my copy of *The Womanly Art of Breastfeeding*, published by La Leche League. It was my guide to being the best mom I could be. And I have wonderful memories!

Being pregnant, giving birth, and caring for babies all involved trips to doctors who wanted to know my medical history and my children's medical histories. For the first time in my life, I realized that someone had been pregnant with me and given birth to me!

In my first adoption memoir (described in Chapter 7), I expressed it this way:

> Becoming a mom awakened my curiosities. I know you'll think this is really weird but I'd never given much thought to my life before I was adopted at 8 months. Giving birth and having a baby to care for made me 'consciously' realize that someone had carried me and given birth to me.

~

I have a large ring binder with all my documents and notes on my adoption story. My search began in 1983. Ron was 5 and Emily was 3.

We visited my parents in Morrisville, Vermont for Easter, which fell on April 3rd that year. I am sure of these details because the first document in my binder is a letter from my dad written on my birthday, April 7, 1983. During our Easter visit, I *finally* pulled myself together and asked my parents if they knew the name of the agency that handled my adoption. I explained that I felt it was important to get my medical history—for myself and the children.

This request marked a milestone moment in my life. It was Easter, after all, and for me, it was a new beginning and a new endeavor. My parents responded with compassion and acceptance. I sensed a little unease from my mother—a slight pause. However, Dad took the lead and immediately assured me that they would get the address for me.

I asked them what information they remembered. Dad described how, when they picked me up at the agency, they were so thrilled to receive me from my foster mother that they never thought to inquire about my birth family.

Our conversation was going well. Then suddenly, I heard myself ask if they knew my name. I hadn't planned on asking for my name, and so it was shocking to hear my mother's quick reply: *"Betty Jean."* She had never once mentioned this during the after-dinner chats so many years before.

My parents had given me family names, Eleanor Mary, but called me "Bonnie" because Dad had always wanted a daughter named Bonnie. Dad knew all about his Scottish heritage. I wonder if they had actually wanted to give me a name somewhat similar to Betty. I was almost 8 months old when they took me home, old enough to know my name.

The adoption agency later informed me that my birthmother named me Betty, not Betty Jean. *"Eleanor Mary, nickname Bonnie"* has been a nuisance over the years. However, I suspect my parents wanted me to have family names, while still having a nickname similar to my given name.

Here is the letter my dad wrote on my birthday in 1983:

Dear Bonnie,

Mary has written to her dear friend, Helen, in the expectation that Helen will be able to obtain an address to which you can write. We'll pass it on to you when received.

You remember Mrs. B., our neighbor in Glenaladale Terrace. She would have been glad to help, we feel sure, but on reflection, we decided that we don't know much about her health and so decided on Helen.

Hope you had a safe trip home, not too tired at the end of it all. Families are far flung nowadays. The house seems quiet!

Love to all,
Dad

Helen responded quickly, and my parents sent her letter along to me:

Dear Don & Mary,

It was a nice surprise to receive your note last week. I hope that Don has been able to get some help with lenses. Dr. Dorothy S. is having the same problem just now.

I phoned this AM to the Ville Marie Social Services and I got the following address for the old Protestant Adoption Center.

Ville Marie Social Service Center

Intake Dept.

5 Weredale Park

Westmount, Quebec H3Z 1Y5

This has not been a good year for skiing, however I did have a few good days on Mt. Tremblant. I understand that they had a lot of snow in the townships last night; too late for me. I am now into the garden and our house is bursting out all over with tomato plants 6 feet high.

I hope that you will drop in & see us if you are up this way this spring or summer. Best wishes to you all.

Love,
Helen

I love Helen's report on ski conditions and tomato plants! She was a wonderful friend; she simply provided the agency address without question or judgments, and moved on to other news.

I, on the other hand, was nervous in anticipation with every communication. This new endeavor of mine was not going to be easy!

Back in 1983, we did not have a computer. We had an old typewriter with an insert correction cartridge that was more trouble than it was worth. I decided to handwrite my correspondences in my best schoolteacher cursive! Here is the first letter I wrote in my search:

May 4, 1983

Dear Ville Marie,

Enclosed are copies of my adoption papers: Notice to the Prothonotary, Certificates of Judgment, Mr. Doxsee's Certification, and my birth certificate. I am interested in obtaining my medical records and other records in my adoption file. I am hoping that the enclosed papers will enable you to locate my records without too much difficulty. It is important to me, now that I am a wife and young mother (my husband and I have a 5-year-old son and a 3-year-old daughter) to obtain these records of my own birth and background.

My parents are supportive of me, and in fact, since they now live in Vermont and I live in New York State, they asked a friend in Montreal to get the address of the Social Services Centre for me.

Thank you for your help. I look forward to hearing from you.

Sincerely,
Eleanor Mary Fairbairn Parsons

I can't help but note my concern that I might have been causing the agency too much difficulty. Am I asking them to do me a favor, even though the records are mine and the information is mine? After all these years, I still occasionally find myself apologizing for inconveniencing someone whose job is to help me.

Then there is the uneasiness of appearing to be ungrateful for my parents who generously took me in. I wanted them to know that my parents were supportive and had obtained her address for me, and that we were a close family. My purpose in writing was simply to learn the circumstances of my birth.

Even today I feel compelled to defend my curiosity about my birth. I recognize that some adoptees, like my sister, are not interested in knowing about their birth and birth families. On the other hand, many adoptees are like me and have a curiosity about their heritage. And I believe we have a right to know.

I appreciated the kind and thoughtful response that arrived later in May, assuring me that they would be sending me information shortly. It was the first in a chain of correspondences with the Ville Marie Social Service Centre, or Ville Marie for short.

~

Ville Marie later became part of the Batshaw Youth and Family Centres. I am including the following statement about the history of Batshaw Centres to clarify the link between Ville Marie and Batshaw. Manny Batshaw was a remarkable gentleman. He believed that each child, unconditionally, needs to be valued and cared for, regardless of his or her age.

> Created in 1992, Batshaw Youth and Family Centres (Batshaw Centres) is a non-profit organization that is part of the Quebec Health and Social Services network. The founding establishments—Ville-Marie Social Service Centre, Shawbridge Youth Centres,

Youth Horizons, and Mount St-Patrick Youth Centre, as well as services offered by the Department of Youth Protection of Jewish Family Services—follow a rich tradition of almost 200 years of service devoted to the welfare of children and their families. Our establishment is named in honour of Manuel G. Batshaw, social worker and renowned activist.

We provide services to children and their families of the island of Montreal who wish to receive them in English and to the Jewish community, in either English or French. We also offer rehabilitation placement services to youths from all regions of Quebec who require them in English.

~

I was prepared to wait a couple of months for the records on my birth. After all, it had taken me a very long time to approach my parents. I had the patience for a couple of months! As it turned out, I didn't have to wait long. I was thrilled to receive a letter from Ville Marie in mid-July.

I went from having no official information to suddenly having all these details! There were so many interesting and amazing details! I was overjoyed and very excited. I've chosen a few key revelations:

YOUR MOTHER:
She was 19 at the time of your birth. A very attractive girl, small and thin, with dark hair and eyes and a medium complexion. She was always very neat, meekly made up and with her hair well brushed. Worker found her quiet and subdued though friendly and easy to talk to. Her mother said she liked to lead.

She went through Grade VI. She had a good job as a clerk with a reputable company who thought well of her.

MATERNAL GRANDFATHER:
He was an electrical draughtsman by profession. An organist at church.

MATERNAL GRANDMOTHER:
She was R.H. negative and lost several babies because of this. She tended to over-dramatize. Very active in church work.

YOUR FATHER:
He was short, of medium build, having a round face.

You weighed 6 pounds 14 ounces at birth, "normal healthy baby."
Your mother called you "Betty."
You were tested at the Mental Hygiene Institute at 24 months and found to be a quiet, friendly little girl, alert, with well-developed visual motor control and coordination.

This letter began a pattern that has continued since July 1983—a pattern of receiving information and then asking new questions based on the information. I now had some pieces to get me started. It would become a giant jigsaw puzzle before I was done!

I recall feeling overwhelmed with everything they sent me, but also with thoughts of my birthmother. I checked out books from the Fairfield Branch of the Buffalo and Erie County Public Library in our neighborhood. I saved the list:

Search by Jayne Askin
The Search for Anna Fisher by Florence Fisher

A Time to Search, author unknown
Jody by Jerry Hulse
Twice Born by Betty Jean Lifton

Day after day, I watched my children play in our little backyard as I read. Something was definitely going on and I didn't know what it was, but *I couldn't get my birthmother out of my mind.*

I wanted to know a myriad of things—including, but not exclusively, medical history. At the core, *I wanted to find my birthmother!*

It would take a couple of years before I understood the reason for the intense feelings I experienced in July 1983.

6

PARENT FINDERS, SEARCH ANGELS

One of the advantages of reading books on adoption is the opportunity to learn about organizations that support and guide birthparents and adoptees in their searches. For example, Florence Fisher wrote *The Search for Anna Fisher* in 1973, the story of finding her original family. This is one of the books I read in the summer of 1983 after my first letter to Ville Marie. Fisher also founded *ALMA—Adoptees' Liberty Movement Association*, a nonprofit organization that still today helps adoptees find their natural parents, and also assists parents in locating the children they relinquished. She talked with Sally Moore of *PEOPLE* magazine back in August 1975 about the identity problems of adoptees. Moore asked Fisher,

What prompted you to start ALMA?

Fisher responded:

It came out of my own search and the realization that I wasn't alone. All adoptees think that there is no one out there who feels as they do. I found that there's a whole underground of people desperate for help, in pain, the way I was. There's a terrible need for communication. A search can be emotionally crippling.

I needed an organization that could help me search in Canada. I had just received the letter from Ville Marie in July 1983 which gave me non-identifying information about my birth families. Then, in August, I learned about an organization in Canada called *Parent Finders*.

I had the opportunity to talk to Candy, the president of the Montreal Branch. Candy and Bev, Director of Correspondence at Parent Finders of Montreal, provided me with guidance and support for the next year and a half.

We went back and forth reflecting on additional non-identifying information from Ville Marie. They guided me by suggesting the next layer of questions. Candy and Bev were my first adoption *search angels*.

Although I never met them in person, I am extremely grateful for their efforts on my behalf. As my adoption angels, they were with me in spirit. And their letters reflected their thorough assessment of my search details along the way.

After our telephone conversation, Candy sent me a letter to get me started. She described the mission of Parent Finders:

CONGRATULATIONS. By contacting an organization like Parent Finders, you've made the first step in a very difficult situation. Parent Finders has two main functions. The first is to try and reunite you with the one you are looking for, and second, to give you lots of moral support, whether through phone calls or personal contact.

I will teach you everything I know about searching, and if I don't know the answer to a question, I will do my best to find you the answer as soon as possible.

I am sincerely looking forward to working with you. I was able to find my mother and hopefully I can help you find your family.

I sent Candy everything she asked for, including the information from Ville Marie containing the non-identifying information on my birth families. Candy responded in August with new questions and suggestions for my next correspondence with Ville Marie:

- Was your biological mother from Montreal? Try to get them to give you a definite city.
- What were the ages and gender of the other children in the home?
- What was the religion of your mother and her parents?
- What was the language spoken in the home?

Phyllis, a Ville Marie Adoption Services Worker, was assigned to respond to my request for information. I wrote to Ville Marie (attention: Phyllis) and asked the questions suggested by Candy.

When she responded, Phyllis ended her letter to me with, "I hope that this information is helpful to you. It is good that you are still close to your adoptive parents." I made sure to address my concern about the phrase "adoptive parents" in my next letter.

Dear Ville Marie,

Thank you very much for your letter concerning my biological parents and relatives. How exciting it was to receive information on my background I've never known before. I appreciate your helpful and understanding attitude in this matter.

I would like to know in which city my biological parents lived, their religion, and language. Also, do you know the ages and gender of my biological mother's siblings?

Concerning my birth, I always had the understanding that I was born in Montreal. Do you have further information, such as time of birth and the name of the hospital? I wonder if my biological mother lived at home for the entire pregnancy and had the emotional support of her parents and siblings.

I'd be interested in any further information along these lines which you uncover and feel free to share with me.

I'd like to comment on the terms used in your letter. I feel they aren't accurate in my situation. I realize every case is different and that you were simply following professional guidelines. My parents are my mother and father in Vermont. I've never used the adjective, "adoptive." I'm seeking information about my birth or biological parents. Perhaps I'm just fortunate that I feel this way. My parents never distinguished their love for their children and I "always" knew I was adopted.

Thank you again for your understanding. I'm looking forward to hearing from you.

Sincerely,
Bonnie Parsons

I also placed an ad in the *Montreal Gazette* personals.

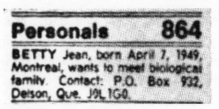

Personals   **864**

BETTY Jean, born April 7, 1949, Montreal, wants to meet biological family. Contact: P.O. Box 932, Delson, Que. J0L 1G0.

However, I never received a response.

Ville Marie got back to me in September 8, 1983:

> We appreciate your comment regarding your parents and are sorry that the term was not used.
>
> In response to your questions, your biological mother lived in Montreal with her family, who was English speaking, and Protestant (Anglican). She stayed with them until entering a maternity home about a month before you were born, and returned to her home following the birth. The siblings were an older sister and two younger brothers.
>
> I am sorry we have no further information on your biological father except that he lived and worked in Montreal.
>
> You were born in Montreal (we do not reveal the name of the hospital), but the hour is not mentioned nor any other details you mentioned, only that you were examined and found to be a normal healthy baby.
>
> I regret that no other information is available.
>
> Yours sincerely,
> Ville Marie

~

I took direction from my Parent Finders adoption search angels and received bits and pieces of information from Ville Marie. Each time Phyllis wrote, she claimed there was no more information.

Thankfully, Candy and Bev helped me probe further after each letter from Phyllis.

I was waiting for Quebec law to change and allow Ville Marie to search for me. Until that time, all they could provide was non-identifying information. At first, I was thrilled to receive mail from Phyllis. However, after a few months, I was frustrated.

In late September, I received another letter from Candy. I am so appreciative of her attention to detail. She was focused on my birthmother, asking me to be patient about my birthfather: "I know that this doesn't seem like much to do, but trust me, it is all very important for the cause. We will try to get all the answers from Ville Marie before we continue down a different avenue. So, until our pipeline is exhausted, we keep asking."

Here are the questions and issues Candy suggested September 28, 1983.

- Was one sister actually older than my birthmother? If so, what was her occupation?
- Verify sisters' and brothers' ages when I was born. Ville Marie had given me different information in their communications.
- Ask if my middle name was Jean.
- Then, did my birthfather know about my birth? What was his reaction?

It is also important to note that Candy was fearless regarding accuracy of the information from Ville Marie. On my own, I might have been hesitant to ask Phyllis to double check the details about my birthmother's siblings.

In October, I wrote to Phyllis. I addressed the issues of my birthmother's siblings and whether or not my birthfather knew about her pregnancy. Finally, I asked for clarification about my middle name, Jean.

Dear Ville Marie,

Thank you for your letter. I appreciate the help and care you've expressed to me.

Please clarify the information about my birthmother's siblings. The first letter said she was the oldest; the second said she had an older sister. If there was an older sister, do you know what her occupation was? I'd be interested to know the ages of my birthmother's siblings when I was born.

Concerning my birthfather, did he know about the pregnancy? If he did, do you have any information about his reaction? For example, did he want my birthmother to continue the pregnancy or not, to keep me herself, or place me for adoption?

Please clarify another point for me. Did my birthmother name me "Betty" or "Betty Jean?" I had been told "Betty Jean" in the past.

Thank you so much for your understanding. I look forward to hearing from you.

Sincerely,
Bonnie Parsons

In December, Ville Marie corrected one error: My birthmother was the oldest of the four children. There was a sister one year younger. I later learned that she was mistaken about my birthmother having two brothers.

And here is a million-dollar statement: "It is not clear in the record whether your biological father was aware of the pregnancy." I am still asking that question! But, why did she say, "It is not clear?"

I found it very interesting that they said, "I hope the above will be helpful." There I was, piecing together the jigsaw puzzle of my biological identity. They had the whole picture on the puzzle box, but only gave me pieces if I asked, and only if they were non-identifying. I still do not understand why the non-identifying information was not complete in the first place, and why they withheld some of it. Perhaps they thought they could satisfy my curiosity with small bits of information!

Candy now turned her attention further to my birthfather. Clearly, she knew that Ville Marie was withholding information I was entitled to. "I know I keep telling you this," she said, "but be patient. Hopefully, it will all pay off in the very near future."

She had a number of concerns for me to address:

- What was the age of my birthfather?
- Was he a professional man like a doctor or lawyer?
- Did he have brothers or sisters?
- Was he married at the time? If yes, was he separated?
- If he was married, did he have any children? If so, what were their ages and gender?

Here is my letter to Phyllis with questions about my birthfather:

Dear Ville Marie,

Thank you for your December 7, 1983 letter. I am very appreciative of your sincere efforts on my behalf.

If there is any information you can share with me in regard to my birthfather, I would be interested. How old was he and did he have any brothers or sisters? Was he married, and if so, was he separated at the time? If he was married, did he have any children, and if so, what were their ages and gender? Finally, was my birthfather a professional—a lawyer or doctor?

Thank you again for being so helpful.

Sincerely,
Bonnie Parsons

Ville Marie replied to me in March, saying, "I am sorry to tell you that there is no information recorded about your birthfather beyond what has already been given, except that he was employed as a motor mechanic. This will be very frustrating for you but I am afraid that there is nothing more to tell you."

I remember thinking, *this is not frustrating for me!* I simply wanted the truth. I had no reason to judge motor mechanics—I appreciate their work! In my adoption story, from early childhood, my birthfather was a lawyer and my birthmother was his secretary. That is why I asked Phyllis if he was a professional. In all fairness, she'd never heard my mom's after-dinner story about my birthparents.

Candy's response regarding Phyllis's letter was handwritten on Parent Finders stationary and difficult to read, so I've typed it.

April 3, 1984

Dear Bonnie,

Hi! Thank you for your letter dated March 14, 1984.

I wish I could say how surprised I was to read Phyllis's letter in connection to your birthfather. Believe it or not, in those years the social workers did not care about the biological father, therefore not many questions were ever asked. It also had to do with the fact that most biological mothers didn't want to talk about the "father," so social workers didn't push in case the woman changed her mind about placing the child with them. It reeks of politics.

My guess is that there is more in your file, but we have to figure it out, and we have to figure out how we ask it. I know Phyllis. When there is nothing left, she'll usually say something like, "Put it behind you and get on with your life!" Knowing Phyllis, it wasn't a final letter. I want you to try and think of other things to ask. Get all of your papers out, go through them with a fine-tooth comb. Ask family or friends to help.

I'm going to do the same from this end. Give me a couple of weeks and Donna (Parent Finders Vice President) and I will see what we can come up with. Write when you have started a list and we'll get going again. I just know there is something we are forgetting, and it's driving me crazy!

I know it's very frustrating. Please be patient with me for a week or two. Thanks!

Take care, Bonnie. I'm anxiously awaiting your next letter.

Sincerely,
Candy

The search process frustrated not only the adoptees but Parent Finders as well. Candy was knowledgeable and experienced. I was impressed that she knew Phyllis. She was also compassionate and anxious to uncover new information for me. Again, why was non-identifying information being held back?

Here are highlights of my response to Candy:

May 7, 1984

Dear Candy,

Thank you for your letter. What a frustration, indeed! I really appreciate your efforts on my behalf and your experience in this area. Perhaps, as I write, you have some new insights.

I'll just more or less list my comments and questions: You were surprised at Phyllis's last letter—because it seemed not to be a final one or because it contained so little about my birth papa? I have a feeling you were expecting she'd give us more, which makes me wonder—is it an uncommonly little bit of information?

The social services had to know his religion! I asked and they didn't answer. With French and Irish parents, he might be Catholic and/or French speaking. Touchy topics then and now!

In her last letter (12-7-83) she says, "It is not clear ..." Do you think something is being withheld here? Why don't they let me make the judgments? Save them the trouble!

Is it likely or unlikely that my birthmother saw and held me?

Do I have a case against "them" because I was never told that my birthmother's mother is Rh negative? Apparently, she lost "several" babies.

Sincerely,
Bonnie

Candy asked for a list of questions and I didn't let her down, but it screams of the frustration in the search process. As an infant, I did not sign up for this!

~

Sometime in May or June of 1984, I called Candy at Parent Finders. Then I followed up with a letter to Ville Marie.

July 12, 1984

Dear Ville Marie,

I have been informed recently by Candy of Parent Finders of a possible change in the law regarding adoptees and birthparents: A Superior Court Judge in Quebec decided that soliciting consent of birthparents is not harassment. Also, at issue is whether or not social service agencies or others will locate birthparents for adoptees. I would appreciate your understanding and opinion on these matters.

I'd be interested in knowing my birthfather's language and religion. Did the social worker meet with him at any time?

How did my birthmother feel about her name and bio-graphical information being given to my parents for my use at a later time?

Thank you for your help.

Sincerely,
Bonnie Parsons

Also in July, Bev wrote back regarding my May 7th letter with questions, as requested by Candy. Bev expressed the same compassion I received from Candy in her support of my search. They were always thoughtful and attentive to every single detail.

Phyllis answered my July letter. She confirmed the Quebec Court Judge's ruling that soliciting consent of birthparents is not harassment. However, she cautioned me not to expect changes anytime soon.

In addition, she clarified a couple of details for me. The social worker did not meet with my birthfather, and my parents were not given any information regarding my birth families. She stated that the information received from my birthmother was utilized to make the best plan me.

~

Throughout my search for information on my birthparents and families, there are gaps in time, sometimes a few months, sometimes years. These gaps often followed my family and work responsibilities, but they also coincided with the slow changes in the Quebec laws and practices and the procedures at Ville Marie.

In December, between Christmas and the New Year, after reviewing the file of all my adoption papers, I wrote my last letter to Parent Finders. Curiosity and frustrations surrounding my family history were once again gnawing at my heart. I am sure this was evident to Candy and Bev. The non-identifying information had been given to me piece by piece with the help from Parent Finders.

Even though these pieces did not divulge family names, they did provide me with pieces to my genealogy puzzle. In my letter, I am so frustrated with not having identifying information that I do not see the value in the non-identifying details. Here are highlights from my letter.

Dec. 27, 1984

Dear Candy and Bev,

I've just reviewed what I know. It's like a little story-book. Without any identifying information, it's all fiction. I've gone around in circles with bits of non-identifying information. Am I ten years before my time? How long will it take to get real help from the courts? Please let me know of any developments in this area. Are there other legal routes—however remote? Are files opened ever in the event of a life-threatening illness? Do I have a case because I was never told that my maternal grandmother was RH negative and had lost "several" babies?

One area we never questioned them about—the group

home my birthmother stayed in, my specific care from birth until adoption, at what time my birthmother signed release papers, and if I was a few months old, did she continue to see me until she gave me up? Can you think of any reason I should ask these questions? Are we quite sure I was born in Catherine Booth Hospital?

Candy, regarding your letter 4-3-84, what were the politics? Why would they care if I was adoptable or not? Also, what kind of final information are we expecting from Phyllis or are we waiting for an error on her part? My mom was the one who told me years ago that my birthfather was a lawyer and my birthmother was his secretary.

I want to put another article in the Gazette on my birthday, 4-7-85. Valentine's Day, too, if you think it's a good idea. Is it possible to submit not just something in "Personals," but a longer, human-interest-type story—main headlines—anything!

I look forward to hearing from you.

Happy New Year!
Bonnie

I was extremely grateful to Candy and Bev. I can hear my *attitude of gratitude*. But I also knew that I was asking for too much from them. My only consolation is that they heard from adult adoptees like me every day. They knew my frustrations only too well.

I wonder if Ville Marie had a strategy for their communications with adult adoptees. Did they see the non-identifying details as hints? For some reason, they did not provide me with all the non-identifying information at the outset of my search. I wondered if I should be waiting for Phyllis to be caught off guard and make a mistake.

Without knowing it, I was onto something!

7

A MOST VALUABLE CLUE

In March the following year, I decided to place another ad in the *Montreal Gazette*. This time, I included my home address. On April 4, 1985, my ad was published:

> *BETTY born April 7, 1949, in Montreal, at Catherine Booth Hospital. Anxious to meet birth family. Mother was 19, one of four children. English-speaking, worked as a clerk. Any information please write: Parsons, address.*

I was unaware that my ad had been printed under "Movers 846" not "Personals 864"—an easy mistake to make considering the number code for each category!

A *very kind* stranger wrote this letter to me regarding the error:

April 11, 1985

Montreal, Quebec

Dear Betty,

Your ad appeared in the incorrect section of the Saturday, April 6th Gazette under "Movers." I am enclosing the Saturday Gazette for your attention. Since you live in Buffalo, I was concerned and notified the Gazette on your behalf. Tuesday, Wednesday, and Thursday your ad was in the correct section.

Are you aware that the law was changed in Quebec in 1984? If you write to the agency that handled your adoption and ask them to search for your birthmother (or family) they will do so.

Most of the old agencies now are handled by Ville Marie Social Service Centre.

If protestant write to:
Ville Marie Social Service Centre
Intake Dept. attention Miss Irani
5 Weredale Park
Westmount, Quebec
H3Z 1Y5
If catholic write to:
Ville Marie Social Service Centre
Adoption Dept.
5835 Verdun Ave.
Verdun, Quebec
H4H 1M1

I am a birthmother making a search and this is why I am concerned for you. I wish you all the best in your own search. You will find that the attitude of the agencies has changed for the better now that they are allowed to make a search. Whomever you write to will acknowledge your letter and I suggest that if you do not receive a reply in 3 or 4 weeks, you write again.

Sincerely,
Joan

A letter from a birthmother named Joan. How thoughtful!

The envelope had no last name or return address. There was no way I could extend my gratitude to her. However, the addresses and information she sent were very familiar to me by now.

My next step was to write to Phyllis at Ville Marie. This would be my last written communication with her. Once she began searching for me, we talked on the phone a number of times.

April 18, 1985

Dear Ville Marie,

Thank you for your last letter to me, dated August 30, 1984. Just recently, I was informed that Quebec law did in fact change in 1984. Please let me know if you are now permitted to search for my birth family with my consent. I would be most interested in knowing about the process, and I heartily give you my consent to search for my birth family.

Thank you for your concern and help. I look forward to hearing from you.

Sincerely,
Bonnie Parsons

~

In the fall of 1989, I agreed to help a cousin, Karen, who was preparing a speech assignment on adoption. I wrote down my story for her—I call it *My First Memoir*. I included details and thoughts about events along the way during the previous five and a half years.

Now, all these years later, I can hear my voice speaking from my heart—recounting the search for my birthmother. I typed that memoir on our Apple IIe computer. The IIe did not have a hard drive; files were saved on floppy discs. At least today, I am copying a typed document, not a handwritten one! Here is the first entry in *My First Memoir*.

October 4, 1989

Dear Karen,

Thanks for the generous phone call. It was fun to catch up as well as to learn about your speech assignment. I'm sure you'll do very well.

I've been trying to figure out the best way to help you. It's all so personal, in that even though others knew I was inquiring, the feelings and motivation were my own. I can give you a chronology, but it is my emotions that mean even more to me. I truthfully wonder if they hold much interest for others. I'll try to summarize and include some correspondences.

Appearance means a lot to adoptees. Who do I look like? And then there is the amazement with parenthood when, for the first time, a relative resembles you!

So, I've included a few photos. I think visuals enhance presentations.

I might add here—and this will surely surprise you and/
or sound weird—as I'd never known a blood relative, after
six weeks of age, that is—it took me a long time, really
years, to stop thinking that Paul was Ron and Emily's
only blood parent. It was just a deep-seated feeling that,
biologically, I was alone. I also felt that Paul's mother (his
dad died in 1970) was their real grandmother, and that
my parents weren't their real grandparents. Again, these
were deep feelings that broke into my consciousness
periodically. The kids are attached to all three grandparents and I don't have these troubling feelings anymore.

Love,
Bonnie

My First Memoir went back to my childhood and events I've
covered in earlier chapters. I'll pick up with the account of
my correspondence with Phyllis in April 1985, after learning
from a birthmother named Joan that the law had changed in
Quebec and that Ville Marie could now assist with searches.
Here is how I explained it to Karen:

I formally gave my consent to Ville Marie for them to
help me. Believe it or not, all my other letters didn't qualify
as consent—my name went on the *bottom* of their list. And
I was told that adult adoptee search was their lowest priority. It is unfortunate that Phyllis did not call or write me.
After all, we had been communicating for over two years.

I thought of contacting lawyers, detectives, and going
to the church where I was baptized for the records. I
talked to local people for help. Every few months I called
Phyllis, my social worker at Ville Marie, to find my place
on the list.

With my parents' help, I first wrote to Ville Marie in May 1983. Then, Parent Finders in Montreal guided me through the search for non-identifying information that hopefully would lead to identifying information! Quebec finally changed the law in 1984, giving the go-ahead for adoption caseworkers to search for birthparents of adoptees, and likewise for children of birthparents. The courts ruled that one phone call from Ville Marie, for example, was not harassment! This was good news, except for the list—I was on the list for two and a half years!

In late 1987, the tide turned in my favor.

I called Phyllis. She had reached me on the list! She said she'd only had a chance to check marriage records and said my birthmother had never married in Quebec. My immediate response was, "Didn't you first check to see if she was alive?" She said she'd call me as soon as she had more information for me.

For some reason, I had the nagging memory of my intense focus on my birthmother back in the summer of 1983. I had been unable to get her out of my mind. I read everything I could get my hands on about adoption searches as I watched my children play on their swings in our little backyard.

January 5, 1988: This was a tough day for me. It was my mom's birthday and I hadn't yet called her. Around 5 p.m., Phyllis called and told me my birthmother had died. Phyllis had spoken to her brother about the details of her illness and said that everyone else was healthy.

Further problems ensued when I told her I still wanted to meet her family and see photos. Phyllis thought she was closing the book on my case, but I had to persist. The law states that one call can be made to a birth parent on behalf of the adoptee. She had died, so the picture changed.

I begged her to contact the family again and see if they would like to meet me.

My First Memoir continues:

Ville Marie and the law–

What followed was a month-long debate on whether or not my birthmother's mother was a next-of-kin. Phyllis was only allowed to talk to next-of-kin. The Ville Marie lawyer said my birthmother's mother wasn't a next-of-kin, that only a husband or children are considered next-of-kin.

As you can imagine, I politely forced the issue. If the person who gave birth to you isn't a next-of-kin, who is? There was no husband. There were no children!

I'd spoken to the lawyer the previous afternoon and had almost convinced him to let Phyllis call my birthmother's home again. I have scribbled notes that add important details—the lawyer told me a court order was needed to authorize a second telephone call. That was "his position" on the matter.

"Little Miss I know who I am and I know where I'm going" made her case politely, with a touch of humor—I told him to "Sleep on it" and "Sweet Dreams!" The next day I asked him how he'd slept! He put me on hold, from Buffalo, NY, and called Phyllis in the next building and gave her the go-ahead. He finally agreed that my birth grandmother was a next-of-kin!

Long distance telephone calls were expensive back in 1988. I remember how strange it felt to be on hold from Buffalo to Montreal. Daytime rates were the most expensive and I had made the call.

After almost five years, I was very anxious to know more about my birthmother and her family. Phyllis made the second call on my behalf and then called me.

My birth grandmother said she wanted to think about everything and talk to her other daughters. She said Phyllis could call her in the summer unless she called first.

Phyllis relayed to me that it was a difficult conversation—dredging up the sad past, the "dirty depression," and all.

This is also when Phyllis let something slip from their conversation. My birth grandmother told Phyllis: "Joan always kept to herself."

~

WOW! My birthmother's first name was Joan! Phyllis had given me a small piece of identifying information! This was the breakthrough I'd been hoping for for so long. Here's how I pieced together everything Phyllis had given me. *My First Memoir* explains:

At this point, I knew that my birthmother died in 1983 of cancer at age 54, and that her first name was Joan. I also knew about other family members and that my maternal birth grandfather was deceased. But I wanted to be patient, and I hoped they would contact me.

Also during this month, January 1988, Phyllis told me that Joan had two other babies after me and gave them up for adoption too. I was shocked to hear this. It changed the picture—or so it seemed. I didn't know what to feel or how to feel. I was really confused. Half-siblings!

How could someone give up three babies? It was beyond my comprehension. The information I received in July of 1983 said that Joan finished grade six. It also said that my birth grandmother's blood was Rh negative and she had lost a number of babies.

The family lived in a small apartment. I learned that four babies were born in the apartment and died shortly after birth due to Grandma's blood type. The last baby, Mary Grace, was born in a hospital and received a blood transfusion. However, tragically, she died at a few months of age, in 1945.

Joan was 16 at the time of Mary Grace's death and only had a grade 6 education. I have thought often about what that must have been like for her, the oldest child. Joan had witnessed her mother's four pregnancies and losses. Mary Grace died in infancy when Joan was a teenager.

I never found out how Joan survived all these traumas. She did not share her feelings with her family—as her mother told Phyllis, "Joan always kept to herself."

Paul said he thought we had enough information to find Joan's obituary in the Montreal newspaper. The identifying information plus the non-identifying information gave us the confidence we needed to drive up to Toronto. Today, we rely on the internet for searches into library archives. In 1988, we hoped to access the *Montreal Gazette* in the Toronto Reference Library. I'm sure I called the library to confirm that they had the Gazette. Toronto is a two-hour drive north from Buffalo. We found the microfilms in the Reference Library and got to work. As I recall, Paul searched the first half of the year and I searched the second half. We were looking for the first name "Joan."

Here is an entry in *My First Memoir* to Karen:

April 5, 1988 — Paul and I decided to drive up to the Toronto Reference Library. We had to go during the

Easter break or wait until July. Our goal was to read the *Montreal Gazette* obituaries on microfilm.

I had a strong feeling that Joan died in the summer, because of all my emotional anguish at the time. Paul started looking at January obituaries. I started with July. It was only right that I should find Joan's obituary, and I did. Joan Helen Williamson, died July 21, 1983.

It was a very emotional event. I learned I'd been Betty Williamson, legally, until my adoption was finalized. We then researched the address and telephone number. I'm summarizing here—we were in the library all day.

Death Notice—

WILLIAMSON, Joan Helen. At the Jewish General Hospital on July 21, 1983, in her fifty-fourth year. Beloved daughter of the late John P. Williamson and Frances Williamson, dear sister of Doreen, Frances, and John. Also dear sister-in-law of Garth. Survived by two nephews and a niece. Dearly missed by dear friend John. Visitation at Clarke MacGillivray White Funeral Directors, 5644 Bannantyne Avenue, Verdun on Friday at 7 p.m. and Saturday and Sunday from 2-5 and 7-9. Funeral service on Monday at St. Clement's Church, Verdun at 2 p.m. Interment at Mount Royal Cemetery. In lieu flowers, donations may be made to the St. Clement's Memorial Fund or to the Canadian Cancer Society and would be indeed appreciated.

I should point out that Joan turned 54 on April 22, 1983. She was, therefore, in her 55th year. Joan's niece, Karen, is my cousin who asked for help with a speech assignment. If it weren't for Karen, I don't know that I would have written my first memoir, which is invaluable to me after all these years! *My First Memoir* continues:

April 6, 1988 — I had trouble getting your phone number or Frances's. My birthday was the next day and I was feeling desperate to connect with my birth family. I finally decided to call the Verdun number and ask if I could talk to one of Joan's sisters. I felt more comfortable with the idea of talking to another woman, and I knew Grandma Williamson wasn't ready or she would have called Phyllis.

I can't remember a time when I've been more nervous. I had a pad ready for note-taking. At the top, I wrote "Don't Hang Up..." a favorite song by the Orlons in the 1950s. I just prayed they wouldn't hang up on me.

I spoke briefly to Grandma Williamson, and then John realized that he should get on the phone. I didn't know they had two phones. Before I knew it, John said, "Hang up the phone," in a firm voice. My life passed before my eyes and I almost hung up in despair. Then he started talking to me, and I realized that he had the extension and had been speaking to Grandma. As it turned out, John couldn't have been kinder to me!

I was still nervous beyond reason, but he was calm and caring. We talked for about twenty-five minutes. I learned a lot about Joan, and John said I could write to him and send pictures of us. That phone call was my first direct contact with my original family since infancy. I had actually talked to someone who knew Joan!

I know this is silly, but didn't Joan work for the phone company? That call never appeared on my bill! Oh, how I wanted to see that phone call on my bill. It would be the written proof that I had talked to Joan's family. I was dying to see it and pay it! I even called the phone company. They had no record of the call. John told me that Joan worked for Northern Electric for thirty-four years. She was a hard worker, well respected, and active in the Northern Electric service organization, the Pioneers Club.

~

When something occurs that seems to be more than a coincidence, it can take our breath away. It's highly personal, but without apparent cause. It is baffling and mystifying. Carl Jung studied this phenomenon and created a term for these meaningful coincidences: synchronicity. I have become more aware of synchronicity during my years searching for my birthparents and families.

Not surprisingly, synchronicity is a common topic in adoption stories. My search angels, as well as the Ville Marie adoption caseworkers, have reported to me that they see highly meaningful coincidences frequently in searches and reunions. In July of 1983, I felt stressed and anxious. I felt an urgency to know more about my birthmother. In Toronto, we discovered that she died on July 21, 1983.

My search began two months earlier, but my file at Ville Marie was tightly sealed, preventing a reunion of mother and daughter from ever taking place.

I was completely stunned when I realized that the letter about my misplaced ad in the *Montreal Gazette* was from another woman named *Joan*, who was also a birthmother, searching for her daughter. She informed me that the Quebec law had indeed changed and Ville Marie could now search for my birthmother. I immediately wrote to Phyllis and finally got on the official list. A truly meaningful and helpful coincidence!

After my parents died in 2000 and 2001, Paul and I drove to Lily Dale, New York. Lily Dale is a community for spiritualists where mediums communicate messages from the departed. I had a private reading with Rose, a registered medium. She explained to me that the strongest loves in our lives come through to her. My mom was present the entire time! Dad was there, too!

Then Rose told me that she doesn't usually accept messages in adoption situations like mine, but my birthmother was present and would not leave. *She wanted me to know that she was sorry she couldn't keep me.* Rose *and* I were stunned!

EMILY AND RONNIE AT JOAN'S GRAVE - JULY 1988

Synchronistic and paranormal events, such as my reading with Rose, share one critical ingredient, and that is love. Even though it is difficult to prove with scientific study, love is what makes a meaningful coincidence meaningful.

In Carl Jung's acausal connection, love is the intangible cause. When we lose a loved one, the love is not lost. We continue to love and adore, and we can feel love in return.

Rose receives and relays messages of love. I am thrilled that Joan's love came through to me. And I'm so impressed and grateful that she persisted with Rose during my reading.

It's easy to be skeptical. At the end of my reading with Rose, she told me that my mom wanted to convince me that it was her, and she was saying, *"Macdonald."* Rose had no way of knowing that I grew up on the Macdonald College campus in

Sainte-Anne-de-Bellevue, Quebec, Canada. It was a jaw-dropping moment. *Okay, Mom, you've convinced me. You're here!*

Ville Marie told me that Joan was required to take care of me for my first six weeks, after which I went into foster care. Joan's brother, John, would eventually give me the document Joan signed on May 27, 1949, relinquishing me to the Children's Aid Society of Montreal.

In 2014, I received my "Summary for the Adopted Person" from Batshaw and read this: "Your birthmother did ask if she could have pictures of you, and she saw you once when you were in foster care. The decision was not easy for her but she felt she was making the best decision for you when she and her parents made an adoption plan."

During that first phone call, John told me much more about Joan. I learned that she could be temperamental. However, she was sentimental and generous. She loved flowers and silk embroidery.

~

Joan had two sisters. Doreen was born in 1930 and Frances in 1933. John was born in 1935. Joan's parents were John Pascoe Williamson and Frances Helen Williamson. Frances is a girl's name, not to be confused with Francis, the boy's name. But it was confused by Ville Marie when they told me Joan had two brothers! Phyllis later corrected the error.

Joan endured two mastectomies. The cancer had spread throughout her body when she died. John took care of Joan in the final stages of her illness. It was truly remarkable to hear him describe what they went through together. He was a devoted brother.

After our call, I wanted to write a follow-up letter to him, which I referenced in *My First Memoir*:

April 8, 1988 — Karen, I wrote to John and I know he won't mind—I'm sending you a copy of it because it expressed my feelings.

Dear Mr. Williamson,

Thank you for talking to me on Wednesday. You were so helpful and kind. I sincerely hope that Mrs. Williamson is feeling better. I was very upset that I had caused her distress. Now that you and I have talked, perhaps she can feel relieved of the burden of having to tell your sisters about me before she is ready. I know I have imposed myself on you, but I truly don't want to cause any further distress. I am going to write to Phyllis at Ville Marie Social Services and ask her not to contact your mother again.

When I decided to inquire about my background five years ago, I wanted my birthmother to know that I was well and happy. I also wanted a medical history for myself and my children. As time went by, and I received information on my family heritage, my natural curiosity increased, and eventually, I wanted to meet my birthmother and her family.

The waiting was frustrating and difficult, but I tried not to worry because she was still young. I now feel a terrible sadness for her suffering and early death, and because we never met again.

Joan gave me the gift of life and then relinquished me to my parents who have always been devoted to me. I have felt for many years that she had the right to know that I was happy and well cared for, even though she gave me up. I have also felt that, if I had the opportunity to meet her, our feelings would in no way diminish or change my love for the family who raised me. My parents and my brother and sister mean the world to me. Now as I write to you, I still hope to see photos and to learn more about

Joan and your family. I really appreciate this opportunity to write to you and I can't stress enough how you helped to put me at ease about making this contact.

I'd like to give you a little information about me. My parents took me home in December of 1949. I don't know who cared for me prior to that. They named me Eleanor Mary Fairbairn and nicknamed me Bonnie. Eleanor and Mary are family names, but my dad always wanted a daughter named Bonnie—as the story goes. So, I went from Betty to Bonnie. We lived in Sainte-Anne-de-Bellevue until I was 13. Then from 1962 to 1970, we lived in Amherst, Massachusetts. On January 17, 1970, I married Paul Parsons who is from Acton, Massachusetts. We lived in Massachusetts and Rhode Island until we moved to Buffalo, New York in 1974. Ron was born in 1978 and Emily was born in 1980.

My favorite hobbies have always been sewing and playing the piano, though much time can pass between inspired moments at either. I also love reading and sports. Paul is a wonderful reader and loves to run. Ron is in 4th grade. He is a good hard worker and absolutely loves sports. He seems to be a natural, particularly at hockey and baseball. He'll soon start his third year in Little League Baseball.

Emily is in 2nd grade. She loves music, putting on little skits to go with songs, and imitating different accents and voices she hears on TV. She roller skates and both kids swim a lot in the summer. Finally, we have two cats that we spoil, Charlie and Cutesie.

In October of 1971, I became a US citizen. I really enjoy living in Western New York. We live in North Buffalo near a large park and the Buffalo Zoo. Ron and Emily have many neighborhood friends. I teach 2nd grade at a suburban school not far from where we live.

I hope this information has helped to remove some of the mystery about me. I am very relieved to have talked to you and I look forward to hearing from you.

Yours sincerely,
Bonnie Parsons

P.S. If you have in your family records, could I possibly have a copy of my birth certificate or hospital records? Thank you, Bonnie

Unfortunately, I misheard John and had written an "8" instead of an "H" in part of the Canadian postal code—it took quite a while for John to receive my letter. But I was no stranger to waits and wrote to him twice in the meantime. Eleven and a half weeks later, I received a phone call from John. But first, here are my letters:

5-10-88

Dear Mr. Williamson,

I hope you received my letter and photos. We're never sure about the time it takes to mail a letter to Canada.

Spring has finally arrived here. The trees are blossoming and everything is so green and beautiful now. Ron plays baseball 3-4 times a week, and he and Emily both play outside for hours with their friends.

I hope the good weather has reached you, too. Is everyone well? Please give my regards to your mother.

Yours sincerely,
Bonnie

6-12-88

Dear Mr. Williamson,

This is a very busy time of year for us. I'm sure it is for you, too. My class put on little puppet plays for some primary classes and their families last Wednesday. It was a creative and heart-warming event. I think the kids were a little less nervous because they were hidden. They had made the puppets, written the plays, painted scenery, and written the program. I was very proud of them. Yesterday we took our annual field trip to the Buffalo Zoo. Parents volunteered to help and we had a beautiful, clear day.

Paul and I have had a most difficult couple of weeks. Our dear friend, Ron, from Seattle, Washington, died in an airplane accident up in Vancouver. We have been close friends since the early 70s in Rhode Island. Our son, Ron, is named after him. We've been deeply shocked and saddened. Life is certainly fragile and precious to us all. I feel we must make the most of our God-given gifts and opportunities.

On July 21st, I wish to take flowers to Joan's grave at the Mount Royal Cemetery. I would love to meet you and your family. I believe our lives can only be enriched by knowing each other. We are not here to judge one another, but to accept and to love.

If you would like to arrange a meeting, please contact me.

Sincerely yours,
Bonnie

On June 27, 1988, John called me! Apparently, Mount Royal Cemetery has strict rules about planting and leaving flowers at grave sites. I could hear the worry in his voice! I quickly assured him that we would abide by the rules and not bring flowers.

Then, I talked to Frances, and I was thrilled. Frances had seen the pictures I sent and thought I looked like Joan. We confirmed plans for our trip to Montreal. After all these years—it was unbelievable. I felt like I was going home. We planned to visit Sainte-Anne-de-Bellevue, too.

8

JOAN'S FAMILY

6-29-88

Dear John,

Thank you for calling me on Monday. It was wonderful to talk to you and Frances. Perhaps she will contact me from Mississauga while your mother is visiting. It is better that she call me because she'll know if your mother feels ready to meet me. In any event, we don't live too far apart and I'm sure we'll arrange to see each other sometime this summer.

My family and I are really looking forward to our Montreal trip. I'm so excited that I don't know if I can wait. And I've never wished away three weeks of my summer vacation before. I made a reservation at Motel Raphael for July 20th and 21st. Ron and Emily will love the pool. Hopefully we'll arrive in the afternoon.

Thank you again for calling. I look forward to meeting you.

Yours sincerely,
Bonnie

July 21, 1988 would mark five years from the day Joan died. Having felt that something was wrong in the weeks leading up to her death in 1983, I couldn't help but wish that things had been different and I'd had the chance to meet her again. From May 1983, when my search began, until her death on July 21, we could have met and hugged and reassured each other. I could have told her I accepted that she wasn't able to keep a baby at age 19. She could have seen that I was happy and doing well. And I could have said, *"Thank you for giving me life."*

My First Memoir captured the feelings I had during our Montreal trip:

July 20, 1988 — Off to Montreal. Such anticipation and anxiety. I called John when we arrived. He came to our motel in the evening. I was almost as nervous as when I'd called in April after our trip to Toronto. It was a most memorable evening. John had a family portrait for me and I picked out Joan. I remember just staring at John as we talked. Poor guy—he was so patient with me. The kids and Paul got along really well with him, too. Then Paul took them to the pool while John and I visited. I asked how he thought Joan would have felt had she been there. John said she'd be the happiest girl in the world. This made me feel better, because I was always afraid of imposing on her family. The truth was I hadn't simply disappeared with adoption, and I really wanted to know about my heritage.

~

John drove us to the cemetery the next morning. Mount Royal is huge and beautiful. It overlooks the city of Montreal. We parked and John used his map to lead us in the right direction. *My First Memoir* explains:

Mount Royal Cemetery — July 21, 1988 — I found my birthmother.

There are hardly words to describe. I was sad and frustrated. My search had begun when Joan was still alive and Ron and Emily were here, too, but Quebec adoption laws kept us apart. I'd tried so hard, but it was too late. And she had suffered so.

Adoption meets a need when babies are babies. But I feel that, as adults, people can meet again. Life is too short to deny people the chance to know each other again. The tide has shifted this way, but it's too late for Joan and me. *She is in my heart.*

I remember writing that--*She is in my heart.* It sounded superficial then, as it does now. She carried me for nine months and gave birth to me and cared for me for six weeks. But the importance and magnitude of these events and the details are lost in a closed adoption. This void of information has caused confusion and angst for me that I hardly know what to do with.

"She is in my heart." That was the best I could do, standing by her grave, never having had the opportunity to meet her again, to know how she felt and how she had handled it all by herself.

Ville Marie had searched on my behalf finally, five years after my initial request. My husband and I had solved the mystery of her identity in the Toronto Reference Library. What an unfortunate tragedy that I found her at Mount Royal Cemetery.

As an adoptee, I found it difficult to ask questions that might upset Joan's family, not unlike my concern for my parents when I wanted to start my search and asked for the name of the agency. Guilt was controlling my mind again! My parents might think I was ungrateful. And now Joan's family might think I was intruding on their privacy. At that time, I recognized my need to know. *Today, I believe it is my right to know.*

Joan's sister, Frances, was probably my best source of information. We kept in touch until she died in 2003. I learned some details from her, but I wish I had probed further. Frances was 15 and living at home when I was born. I know Joan's pregnancy was very hard on her. Why didn't I ask her what life was like in their small apartment during Joan's pregnancy? How did everyone cope with it?

I believe Joan spent the last month of her pregnancy at Catherine Booth Hospital before my birth. Did anyone visit her there, either before or after I was born? Did Grandma Williamson or anyone else see me or hold me?

When I met Joan's family in 1988, I had no idea that Joan had visited me in foster care and had asked for pictures of me. I had not been told that the adoption decision was difficult for her, and that she did not give her consent until October 12, 1949, when I was over six months old.

I experienced only one time in my life when I felt Joan's presence unequivocally and the need for us to be together. That time was in the summer of 1983, when Joan was dying.

I'd started my search in May and in July, I received the first letter from Ville Marie containing non-identifying information about Joan and her family. I spent hours reading books on adoption, memorizing every detail of the non-identifying information, and feeling a sense of urgency to find her.

On July 21st, at the Jewish General Hospital in Montreal, Joan died from breast cancer. Ironically, my search was just beginning.

Almost twenty years later, Joan was finally able to communicate with me through Rose at Lily Dale—she wanted me to know she was sorry she couldn't keep me.

~

It took us a while at Mount Royal Cemetery to find Joan's gravestone. Even with John's map, the cemetery is huge and confusing. Sadly, the gravestone also had John's name and the year of his birth and a hyphen. Doreen was married and would be buried next to her husband, Garth. And Frances lived in Mississauga, Ontario. So, there was a logic to including sister and brother, Joan and John, on one gravestone.

We laid our hands on the gravestone and took photos. Then we looked further until we found Grandpa Williamson's stone. He died the year before Joan, in February 1982. Grandma's name and year of birth were next to his. She was a healthy 82 at the time.

While in Montreal, we visited the apartment where they lived! So many details are flooding my mind! It was on the second floor, at the top of a long, narrow staircase. John had a small room at the front and there was a balcony overlooking Wellington Street. The living room and small dining room had many family treasures and photos. There were prints by the *Group of Seven,* Canadian landscape artists that were also my parents' favorites!

BONNIE AND JOHN

There were two bedrooms—one for Grandma and the other had been Joan's. I imagine the girls all shared the room John now called Joan's room. I took a couple of steps into the room--but I became very anxious feeling Joan's presence surrounding me. John encouraged me and invited me to stay anytime. I recall hearing him, but the thought of sleeping in that room was completely overwhelming and simply terrifying for me.

This was the apartment where Joan, Frances, Doreen, and John were raised. Grandma Williamson had Rh negative blood. After John's birth, she'd had five more pregnancies. Due to the Rh negative factor, four babies were born and then died in the apartment.

The last baby, Mary Grace, was hospitalized and had a blood transfusion. She lived for a few short months and died in 1945. Doreen told me that she remembers pushing Mary Grace in the baby carriage on Wellington Street with her sisters.

The day after our visit to the cemetery, John came with us to Doreen's house in St. Lazare, west of Montreal. Doreen was very sweet and I was thrilled.

BONNIE AND DOREEN

Grandma Williamson and Joan's siblings knew about her pregnancies. They also knew that the call might come someday from one of Joan's children. It was a close-knit family. Even though Joan was a private person regarding her own difficulties and deepest emotions, she was close to her parents and siblings.

FRANCES, DOREEN AND JOAN

Doreen told me that, whenever she mentioned to Joan that she needed help with her children or the housework, Joan was there for her--sentimental, generous, and hard working.

I know Joan's cancer and death at such a young age were heartbreaking for her family. But now, after five years, they had the opportunity to meet Joan's first born. At the cemetery, John said that he thought he was looking at Joan, as I stood a short distance from him. Our resemblance was striking to him.

Joan's family always knew I was out there somewhere. When we met, they loved me and my family as part of their family. Frances later said that Joan and I had the same hands and handwriting. Doreen signed all her letters, "Always thinking of you. Love, Doreen." To this day, she and I sign off our chats with, "I love you."

Joan was no longer with them, but my presence, in a way, brought her back. She was a daughter, sister, aunt, and my birthmother. As we got to know one another, her family and I felt closer to Joan.

Doreen wrote me following our trip. The card has a beautiful cat on the front. We'd discovered very early on that we were both cat families.

Dear Bonnie,

First of all, here is the recipe for Banana Bread. Hope you like it. Remember I use Eggbeater where it calls for eggs.

It was nice meeting all of you, although, as you say, a bit short.

I've been very busy with my babysitting. I also get a lot of knitting done while I'm sitting, so I've started to make Christmas presents.

I don't know if I told you that Joan was a very hard worker, when something had to be done, you can be sure it was done. I still miss her very much. Whenever I had a lot of work, she would come for a weekend and help me.

Well, Bonnie, as I told you, I'm not much of a letter writer, but I'll try. I must go now, got a lot of work to do. You've got a nice family. Maybe someday we will meet again.

Love to all of you,
Doreen

~

In August, a couple of weeks after our trip to Montreal, I received a call from Phyllis at Ville Marie. I'm sure I updated her about finding Joan's last name in the Toronto Reference Library and about our trip to Montreal. I took notes on new bits and pieces of information she gave me from my adoption file.

> During her pregnancy: Joan came in with her father. Agency then went to their home for a visit and met her mother. Joan was discharged from Catherine Booth on May 20th. Agency saw Joan only *after* the other births. Boy born 4-53, adopted 1-54. Girl born 4-55, Roman Catholic father.

In August, I received a call from Frances. I wrote this note in return:

August 18, 1988

Dear Frances,

I'm so happy you called. I've been looking forward to meeting you for a long time. How kind of your friend to come along. Did she ever meet Joan?

I was very nervous and almost fearful when I met John and Doreen. Just the memory of it brings tears to my eyes. For adoptees, searching and meeting one's natural or original family is a very emotional event. There is so much risk. And for that reason, I tried to keep my expectations low. But now that I've met John and Doreen and her family, their warmth and kindness have taken away many of my fears. Everything that happened in Montreal far exceeded my hopes and dreams. It was such a special time for me. Although today is only the 18th, I think by the 27th I'll be more excited and not as afraid to meet you!

I'd love to see photos and letters. I'm curious about her handwriting.

Thanks again for getting back to me.

Until the 27th,

Yours sincerely,
Bonnie Parsons

On August 27th, Frances and her friend, Jean, came to our house in Buffalo for the first time. Here is the entry in *My First Memoir*:

Karen, August 27, 1988—Frances and her friend Jean came to Buffalo for the day. We shared photos, handwriting samples, and visited all day! It was truly another super day. With each new acquaintance, I felt I knew more about Joan.

During our lunch together, Frances excused herself and went to the powder room. When she returned, she said, "I came here knowing there were four babies!"

Joan gave birth to three of us at Catherine Booth Hospital in Montreal: in 1949, 1953, and 1955. Phyllis first gave me that information on my mom's birthday January 5, 1988, when she called to tell me Joan had died.

GRANDMA AND FRANCES VISIT US. PAUL, BONNIE, GRANDMA, RONNIE, FRANCES & EMILY

And now Frances knows about a fourth baby! Frances explained that, starting in the 60s, Joan had a boyfriend, Johnnie, who lived on a farm in Hemmingford, south of Montreal. Joan spent her weekends with him. Around 1969, at the age of 40, Joan gave birth to a baby girl and named her Shirley. Frances and the Williamson family thought that Johnnie was the father. He is included in Joan's death notice. "Dearly missed by dear friend John."

I wrote to Doreen in September in response to her note after our trip to Montreal—

September 10, 1988

Dear Doreen and Family,

Thank you for your letter and the banana bread recipe. What a treat for us! I don't bake often but we all love banana bread.

You sure sound busy with all the babysitting. Now that school has started, do you care for children after school until their parents are out of work? Those are lucky kids to have you!

I appreciate you telling me about Joan being a hard worker. It makes me feel so proud. I know now what a strong family I came from. I was talking recently to a friend who was also adopted. I told her that I could have continued to live happily if I hadn't found all of you but... And she said, "But, now your life is richer." And she's right. My life is so much richer. I know where I'm from and I have pictures of Joan and all of you that warm my heart. I know why I look the way I do, traits I have inherited, and why I work so hard.

My parents have always been very proud of me. I know they are pleased that I wanted to work hard and graduate. They were also thrilled that I loved the piano so much and often sewed my own clothes.

Giving up a child for adoption is traumatic for all involved, but when time passes and it works out, I feel people can benefit from meeting one another. I feel that Joan had a right to know I was healthy and to meet me if she wished. She has given me such a wonderful—not to mention challenging—life, and I am so grateful. I take nothing for granted.

Frances and Jean visited us two weeks ago. Talk about nervous, but I wasn't as bad as in Montreal and with you. I actually walked out to greet them! We talked and ate all day. And it was a wonderful day. I tried to show them around a bit—where we work, the kids' school, and our prettiest downtown marina.

We talked a lot about Joan. Frances brought photos and gave me a beautiful one of her and two of "the three sisters in their Christmas aprons." One is a close-up and it's my favorite of Joan. Frances also brought a recipe Joan had written--we were all amazed at the similarity with my handwriting. We agreed that Joan was smiling down on us, approving of our visit.

Please give John my love from all of us and your mother, too. I look forward to when she and I meet—it will be such a special day.

P.S. Worrier that I am, I want to clarify my feelings about school. I know Joan went to 6th or 7th grade. And certainly, you don't have to go to school to prove you are a hard worker. I think that what Joan gave me was a strong will to work hard and finish things you start.

~

In November 1988, I wrote a letter to Johnnie, Joan's dear friend, in which I introduced myself, gave him a bit of my backstory, and so on. The following are some of the highlights:

Dear Mr. Walker,

I have looked forward to writing you since last summer, but not without considerable nervousness. Now on this vacation day following our Thanksgiving, I'm going to give it a shot. I hope you will feel happy about this correspondence, because I have no intention of interfering in your life at all.

I was born at Catherine Booth Hospital April 7, 1949. Last January '88, I learned that my birthmother's name was Joan. I am aware that you met her sometime later. Ville Marie Social Services in Montreal inquired on my behalf and the social worker I've been in contact with since May of 1983 finally called and told me that Joan had died. Joan's brother, John, told the social worker about the cancer, and she passed this sad news on to me. They still wouldn't give me Joan's last name or any other "identifying information."

After waiting patiently for so long only to find out that Joan was still alive when I had first asked about her, my husband and I decided to get more information on our own [which we found during the Easter vacation last year, in her obituary, on microfilm in the Toronto Reference Library]. This was a very emotional event for me. Adoptees are often treated as second-class citizens when they want information, and yet on our own we finally learned my birthmother's full name and my original last name. I already knew Joan named me Betty. The paper mentioned you as a dear friend and I was relieved to know she had you. I have hoped that eventually we could meet. I am interested in knowing people who knew her. It warms my heart. From what Doreen, Frances, and John have said, Joan and I are similar in appearance and personality.

I contacted the Williamsons after our trip to Toronto. In July, my family and I went to Montreal. I wanted to visit Joan's grave on the 21st, five years after her death. We made plans ahead with John and he was extremely kind and generous throughout our two-day stay. Mrs. Williamson was visiting Frances in Mississauga. The evening we arrived, he came to our motel and had a family portrait to give to me. We had no trouble picking out Joan. Our glasses, hair, and posture are the same. I even have a similar dress. I don't have the words to express my feelings about our trip. I'm almost 40 and I'm learning about my heritage. It was awesome just to be in the Verdun flat, and to look around and see pictures of others with the same square jaw.

In August, Frances visited us in Buffalo with her friend, Jean. Jean is from Montreal and now lives in the same building with Frances in Mississauga. We talked and looked at photos all day. I also showed them around our town a bit. It was another emotional time! Frances took pictures and sent a set to us and to her mother. I look forward to meeting her mom—perhaps next summer when she visits Frances.

My sister, who was also adopted, had an unplanned pregnancy in 1968 and gave up her baby son for adoption. My family has experienced adoption from both sides. The feelings are traumatic no matter how you look at it. In my search, the most difficult aspect has been adjusting to Joan's death and the fact that we'll never see each other again. All other aspects, though highly emotional, have been positive. I'm repeatedly scared silly and then things work out.

My birthfather was a "motor mechanic" in 1948-9. He was "short, medium build and had a round face." If you know anything about him—then or now—please let me know. I want the other half of my medical history, and I'll be as discreet as always

In January, after learning that Joan had died, the social worker also told me that Joan had other children. I want you to know that I know about them so that you won't feel that you have to either keep secrets or shock me. I think you will find that I'm not the type to pass judgments on others, in fact, I usually have quite an optimistic view of life.

I asked John about you when we were in Montreal. He said you lived in Hemmingford and that you haven't seen each other in a while. Since his mother hasn't yet met me, I'd prefer that you not call them. She's 83 now and accepting my search at her own pace, which is her right. John gave me your name without my asking. He and the others had very kind words to say about your relationship with Joan. I hope you'll accept my contacting you with the same kind feelings I'm sending, and not wish that John had kept your name from me. I'm sure he didn't intend to break your confidentiality. Anyway, I'm here and I'm harmless!

Hoping to hear from you soon.

Sincerely yours,
Bonnie Parsons

When I did not hear back, I called Johnnie in December. We had a very pleasant chat, and I still have my scribbled notes. He has an adult daughter in Mississauga. He and Joan met in the 60s. Joan was a pay clerk at Northern Electric. She had the best attendance record.

Johnnie and Joan loved the farm--they had animals and a vegetable garden.

In the late 1960s, Johnnie was stationed way up north in Schefferville, Quebec on assignment with the Canadian Navy. He explained to me that, when he returned after a number of months, Joan was pregnant. He did not know who the father was, but it couldn't have been him.

Johnnie made a point of telling me that he stood by Joan. The baby girl was born at the Barrie Memorial Hospital in Ormstown, one town over from Hemmingford. Her adoption was private. He did not judge—he was simply there for Joan. Johnnie talked about Joan's cancer and her mastectomies. She got depressed, he said, but she was a fighter. At the end of our call, he said, "Joan was very good to me."

I will always cherish that conversation. Johnnie and Joan shared a caring and supportive love. They were blessed to have each other.

JOAN IN HEMMINGFORD

Joan gave birth to four babies. I was born in 1949, a baby boy was born in 1953, another girl in 1955, and finally a baby girl around 1969. Each baby was relinquished and adopted.

Seven years later, in 1977, Joan began her battle with breast cancer. She lost that battle in 1983—but not until she had suffered surgeries and heartbreaking debilitation as the cancer spread. Johnnie and Joan's family did everything they could do for her, but it was too late to stop the cancer.

9

ORIGINAL BIRTH CERTIFICATE

My parents had a couple of documents relating to my adoption, such as the *Certificate of Judgment*. I think I was in my thirties when they gave me these documents.

When we moved to Baltimore for a year, they got a birth certificate for me, issued on December 27, 1961. They are named as my mother and father. The seal is not embossed, and the registration date is January 16, 1948, even though my date of birth is correct—April 7, 1949. I wish they'd had it corrected!

In the fall of 1988, after our first trip to Montreal, I decided to try and get my original birth certificate (OBC). My notes indicate that I first called a Montreal Court House. A nasty voice told me my OBC was *top secret,* that I had a *new identity,* and referred me back to Ville Marie.

Next, I wrote to the Municipal Services, Archives Division at Montreal City Hall. This time I did *not* mention adoption!

October 17, 1988

To Whom It May Concern,

Please send me a copy of my Birth Certificate. My name is Betty Williamson Parsons. My mother's name is Joan Williamson. I was born April 7, 1949.

Enclosed is a money order for $8.00 Canadian funds made out to the Minister of Finance.

Thank you.

Sincerely,
Betty Williamson Parsons

November 22, 1988—I received the following letter:

re: birth certificate.

Dear Madam:

Following your letter, we regret to inform you that we cannot give further consideration to your request, because you were not registered at Montreal City Hall.

However, we forwarded your request and your money order to the Provincial Archives, Court House, 1 Notre-Dame Street East, Room 1.140, Montreal, QC. Canada H2Y-1B6.

We trust that this will prove satisfactory to you and wish to remain,

Yours truly,
Division Manager

The first sentence was disappointing until I read further. The Provincial Archives Division came through for me with a copy of my OBC dated December 8, 1988. It is amazing! It has my name and Joan's name and her signature. This is the kind of error I love!

I shared this story not long ago with a Batshaw social worker. She let me know immediately that someone had made a mistake. They should have checked for adoption!

Phyllis made the first mistake back in January, accidentally quoting Grandma Williamson: *"Joan always kept to herself."* This was the piece of identifying information I needed to find my birthmother. Now due to a second error, I received my original birth certificate. It is against the law in Quebec to give adoptees their original birth certificates.

～

Although I knew my OBC belonged to me, I didn't fully understand the moral implications and the need for a change in the laws that keep adults from knowing their original identity. Now that I have a greater understanding, I am more disheartened than ever.

It's ironic that ancestry.com helps people with their family trees going back many generations. For most people, their searches begin with themselves and their own identity! However, adoptees, *by law*, are forbidden to know their identity, and therefore, they have no way of discovering past generations and building an authentic family tree.

I read as much as I can. In fact, I paused my work on this memoir to have a reading break, much like a college reading period between semesters. I read books and blogs and reader comments. I applaud the leaders in the movement working to change adoption laws. I follow the progress on social media every day. It is a moral injustice to deny an adult his or her identity.

～

I wrote *My First Memoir* to help Karen, Doreen's daughter—it ends in December 1989. This is the entry I wrote on the last page regarding my original birth certificate:

> Karen, Birth Certificate—I feel this and other documents concerning me belong to me (copies of originals, if necessary). Adopted babies grow up to be adults with civil rights. Last winter I finally got the nerve and sent away for my birth certificate saying I was Mrs. Betty Williamson Parsons. I expected to get nothing, as I thought the records would indicate adoption. But they sent it to me! It is the only document I have that links Joan and me. It has my date of birth, my birth name, and her signature.
>
> Earlier in my search, I'd contacted Catherine Booth Hospital, figuring that's where I had been born. *Apparently*, there was a fire around 1949 or 1950 and all hospital records were burned. They had only been able to confirm that Joan Williamson gave birth to a baby girl on April 7, 1949. I'll never know the time of my birth or details of the first six weeks when Joan cared for me.
>
> Well, Karen, there you have it.
>
> I know it takes two to tango, but I don't have any clues about my birthfather or half-siblings. And I need a break.
>
> I appreciate tremendously everything your family has done for me. We can't bring Joan back, but I now know where I'm from and I have a good sense of what Joan was like.
>
> Good luck on your project.
> Love, Bonnie

I am very grateful that Karen asked me to share my story with her. This early memoir refreshes the details of events and my feelings throughout the search process. Karen did well on her adoption paper. In addition to my memoir, she said, "I also read quite a bit about adoption, and I realize that to put a child up for adoption is a very emotional time for the parent, and Aunty Joan did what she thought was best for her child."

But there were three more children! Joan relinquished four babies. I can only imagine the heartache she suffered. Her brother, John, and Johnnie Walker each mentioned her bouts of depression.

The entire family said that she was very private and never shared her deeply personal feelings. Signing consent for the adoption of one baby is overwhelming and life-changing, but four? Had she lived to meet me, would she have shared her feelings with me?

Joan's apology expressed through the medium, Rose, at Lily Dale, was stunning. Joan was there! And she insisted on saying that she was sorry she couldn't keep me. I was so shocked that I didn't know how to respond. Today I would say, *I love you. I want you to know I am okay.* Maybe I would also say, *I have never been angry with you. You have grandchildren and great-grandchildren! I hope to see you again someday.*

10

REUNIONS AND BLOODLINES

When I planned the trip to Montreal to visit Joan's grave in July 1988, I had never heard the term "adoption reunion." Today there are definitions of terms, casts of characters, and directions to help families and adoptees reunite. Reunions can go in many directions, both good and bad. As I reflect on my adoption reunion experience, thirty years later, I'm more appreciative than ever for the wonderful reunion I had with Joan's family.

Doreen recently shared a conversation she had with Grandma Williamson after our reunion. Grandma said that I looked so much like Joan that I brought back too many sad memories, and it was upsetting for her. When asked how she would react if asked to meet another one of Joan's adult children, she said, "I won't do that again!"

I am sorry I caused Grandma distress--she lost her firstborn to cancer, and I arrived on the scene only five years later. However, Grandma and I shared our lives for fifteen years, from 1988 to her death in 2003 at the age of 96. We had wonderful visits and always signed our cards and letters with love. My reunion with Joan's family was facilitated by her brother,

John. Our reunion in Montreal and Saint-Lazare could not have been more appropriate and wonderful!

Yes, I apparently upset her—but, I didn't choose to be taken away from Joan at the age of six weeks. I didn't choose to have my identity sealed and locked away forever. When I was a newborn, decisions were made for my care that permanently changed my identity. The cultural mores dictated that Joan had sinned and I was illegitimate. She was a disgrace to her family and her community. This disgrace should not have played a part in the adoption plan, but tragically, it played a major role. I was a healthy, happy little baby girl who would have chosen to be with her mother. Unfortunately, we had to be separated. Forever.

If the community, or society for that matter, had been supportive of unwed mothers, Joan and I would have had a chance to stay together. She was an adult, turning 20 only two weeks after my birth.

Joan's brother, John, was so welcoming and I was patient with Grandma. She wasn't ready to meet me and told Phyllis that my birth reminded her of the *dirty depression*. In time, she came around. And I believe she would have again if another one of Joan's babies had called.

To date, I have not heard from my half-siblings, although I did hear from the daughters of two of them. Someday, I hope to hear from them directly, and at that time, I will share everything I've learned about our heritage that they wish to hear.

～

Joan brought great shame upon her family. There was no joy in her pregnancies, congratulatory cards or gifts, no clamoring to hold a newborn, chatter about whose eyes and hair color the baby has, no family pride in the next generation of

Williamsons. Doreen said Grandma *might* have visited Joan and me at the hospital. But, certainly, no one else visited.

How in the world did Joan handle the shame? How did she cope with the hormonal changes having just given birth, knowing she would now be expected to relinquish me? And lastly, what was the effect of these circumstances on a newborn? I pray we had peaceful and loving moments together.

I've never understood, and certainly never liked, shame. My parents were part of the generation that believed children should be seen and not heard. My mom's mantra was, "Shame on you," or "You should be ashamed of yourself."

Society said that unwed mothers were somehow a lower class, and that the best thing for their babies was to be adopted by a married couple. We know this is not necessarily true, but it used to be the norm. Why were unwed mothers and their babies shamed and not cared for?

In the United States, birthmothers can still sign consent for termination of their parental rights immediately, or even before the baby is born. The truth, however, is that birthmothers need time to recover from delivery. They also need time to make the best decisions for themselves and their babies.

One unfortunate cause for this lack of support in the United States is that adoption is a lucrative business. When the adoption industry supports lawmakers, it is difficult to get the laws changed to support unwed mothers and babies. Again, I applaud adoption-reform advocates. We need to change the laws. It is immoral and harmful to deny birthmothers and infants support in order to preserve a profitable industry.

~

First, mother and infant are shamed. Then their identities are severed from each other. Identity is sacred! Sealing an infant's identity in a vault somewhere and replacing it with a different identity is immoral and should be illegal, in my opinion. This is a civil rights issue!

While in foster care, the infant has the name given by her mother. I was Betty Williamson for 8 months. Once the adoption is finalized, a new birth certificate is issued. The baby's original name and parents' names, often just the mother's name, as in my case, are replaced with the baby's new name and the adoptive parents' names. It is a *birth* certificate, but the birthmother's name is removed--original birth certificates should never be sealed. In an adoption, a new certificate should be issued with the adoptive parents' names and the baby's new name.

When I first heard the analogy of the loss of identity in adoption being like the loss of identity in slavery, I was shocked and troubled by it. Could this really be true? I needed time for this to sink into my soul.

My friend and mentor, author Lorraine Dusky, addressed the comparison in her blog, back in 2009, long before I'd heard about it. Below, she is describing the contract in a closed adoption like mine. After a couple of readings, it is clear to me—still troubling, but very clear. I am beginning to understand. This comparison is *not* about racism and the tragic circumstances of slavery. It involves contracts and an individual's identity.

> But save slavery, there is no other contract in the world in which two parties (the birth/first mother and the state) enter into which so affects and controls the current and future status of a third party—the one who is adopted—without any input from her or him. The contract between the birth mother and the state destroys the legal and real identity of the individual in most states for all eternity. The contract does not have a term limit, nor can it be changed when the adopted

individual becomes an adult. The state upholds the contract, considers it a legal document that must take precedence over any desires of the third party, the one about whom the contract was written. How is this not like slavery?

∽

In closed adoptions, parental rights are severed, too. Birthmothers suffer heart-wrenching grief and babies are separated from their mothers and biological families. Searches often go on for decades, and in the end, that time can never be recovered.

Philomena: A Mother, Her Son, and a Fifty-Year Search by Martin Sixsmith, and the movie by the same name, describes the grief and pain felt by an Irish mother and her two-year-old son who were suddenly and abruptly separated for the purpose of his adoption by an American couple. It is a moving testimony to the strength of the mother-infant bond and a child's sacred identity.

I have mentioned before that Joan was alive when I began my search for her. I wrote my first letter to Ville Marie requesting information on May 4, 1983. Joan was still at home. She was hospitalized for the last time June 25, 1983 and died July 21, 1983. She was only 54 and strong enough to fight the cancer right to the bitter end. From May to July, we could have shared valuable time together.

∽

Joan endured so many tragic losses—her mother's five infants, her own relinquishment of four infants, her father's death, and in the end, breast cancer. She could be temperamental and suffered from depression. I secretly wondered if our reunion would have been traumatic. What if she felt too much like a stranger to me?

But over time, I imagined it differently. Joan was nearing the end of her life. She was fighting through pain and cancer treatments. I wish Ville Marie had called their house when they received my letter in May 1983 and asked to speak to her.

I now believe that Joan and I would have had a touching reunion. We would have looked into each other's eyes and felt a closeness. In remembering, we would have renewed our mother-daughter bond. She may have been comforted by my presence. Some of the shame may have washed away. After all, she gave me life, and I have two children and four grandchildren, her grandchildren and great-grandchildren! I believe my gratitude would have been accepted in her final days. In the limited time, we would have focused on each other and appreciated our time together.

~

What is it like to be relinquished? I've read about the loss felt by infants like myself and my sister before we had the language skills to express our feelings. These *implicit memories* are formed from our experiences and our emotions, but they cannot be expressed with language until we are a little older.

It was common for babies to be separated first from their mothers and then at least once from foster mothers and families, depending on the number of placements they had. Joan relinquished me at six weeks, and I went into foster care until I was almost 8 months old.

I feel I have emotional memories of my separations from Joan and my foster mother. I believe these early experiences influenced the way I reacted in situations, such as my sheer terror when I was 8 and the ambulance came for my dad and took him out on a stretcher. And similarly, when my mom said after a day at the hospital, "We almost lost your father today." Terror is not an overstatement.

One of my earliest explicit memories is a recurring nightmare I had when I was quite young, I believe around 3. In the nightmare, my wrists are bleeding. I can still picture the gruesome scene. When I got a little older and woke up shaking from a bad dream, I would have those *quiet conversations* with myself in front of the bathroom mirror until I was calm enough to return to my bed and get back to sleep.

From my reading and soul-searching, I also know with all my heart that Joan suffered terribly when she had to make the *adoption plan*, and I know that I desperately wanted to stay with her and was taken from her. I take comfort from Joan's presence with the medium, Rose, at Lily Dale. I also believe what John said to me in July 1988, "If Joan were alive today, she would be the happiest girl in the world."

My reunion with Joan's family was amazing. For the first time in my life, I saw similarities between my appearance and abilities and those of my biological relatives. I learned that someone on Grandma Williamson's side was a seamstress for the British royal family! Grandpa Williamson played the piano and was the organist at St Clement's Anglican Church in Verdun. Sewing and playing the piano are two of my favorite things to do from a very young age.

Doreen told me how her parents loved music and dancing. My Agency Adoption Summary says that at ten months, "You enjoyed music and listening to the radio."

~

The Williamson family went to church weekly and believed in volunteerism. Grandma served as president of the Women's Association for over twenty-five years. At the age of 86, she received an award from Anglican Bishop Andrew Hutchison of Montreal as an outstanding lay person in the diocese.

GRANDMA WITH HER AWARD

As a child, I wanted to go to church and be in the choir and youth groups. Around the age of 14, I was eager to attend a springtime sunrise service, which I assumed would take place at our church, about a mile away. This is an embarrassing story. Note to self--always check out event details beforehand! I was determined to get up quietly and sneak out of the house without disturbing my family. I was really looking forward to the sunrise service. I even remember the colorful Easter dress I chose for the occasion.

However, as I approached church, I could see families and cars in the parking lot, and there was not one pretty dress in sight! People appeared to be wearing hiking clothes and boots. Somehow, I survived my embarrassment. A kind family offered me a warmer coat and a ride, as it was a cold and damp morning. The service was out of town on a beautiful hill overlooking a valley. It never occurred to me that the service would be outdoors, but there I was. And the sunrise was beautiful.

As a young adult, I served as a Deacon in my church for six years and on the Caregivers Committee. As caregivers, we provided rides to and from church and delivered food baskets. We visited folks in the hospital and in their homes.

Grandpa Williamson was an electrical draughtsman. He helped draft the design for the Confederation Bridge between Prince Edward Island and New Brunswick. I believe he loved detail and was patient with his work. When I was a year and a half old, the summary states, "You had a gentle demeanor and handled things carefully."

~

In December 1950, I was seen for the last time by the agency; "...you were described as friendly, active, smiled and played happily with your toys and your brother."

I have no doubt that losing Joan and my foster mother were traumatic events in my life. However, if I can believe the accuracy of the agency reports, Joan and my foster mother gave me the love and security I needed to adapt to my new family life.

By December 1950, I had been with my family for an entire year. Four months later, I turned 2. Joan turned 22. I try to imagine myself in the Williamson apartment. John was only 16 that year, Frances was 18, and Doreen was 21.

IAN AND BONNIE - 1950

Most certainly, I would have been a burden to Grandma while Joan was at work, and a disgrace to the entire family. After all, I was illegitimate—an unwanted pregnancy.

In 1949, there were no options. Adoption was not the last resort, it was the only resort. Today, Joan would have options, including birth control and abortion.

The Williamsons knew about me and my siblings. Even though adoptions saved them from public shame, they knew that Joan's babies were biologically related to them, that we were part of the family. This knowledge provided the foundation for our reunion. They had accepted me before we met. Immediately, they loved me unconditionally, as if I was lost and now found.

They were genuinely interested in me and my family. I know that Joan's pregnancy and my birth had been traumatic for everyone. Frances told John that I was the reason she never married or had children of her own. But after almost forty years, I was warmly welcomed into their family. I was blessed to experience a loving reunion, and I am so very grateful.

Following our reunion, there were numerous letters, gift exchanges, and phone calls. John was always welcoming and helpful. He added my name to a family tree document he prepared. I corresponded with Grandma, Doreen, Frances, and her friend, Jean, through letters and cards. We sent flowers to Grandma each year on her birthday, and she sent us thank you notes and enclosed photos of the bouquets.

Our two cats were always included in correspondences. One cat family to another! Doreen's daughter, Karen, and I had a special relationship—once she got over the fact that she wasn't the only granddaughter! We exchanged many letters and photos, not to mention the memoir I wrote to help her with her school assignment. She sent me a photo of her Aunty Joan following chemotherapy treatments.

JOAN AFTER SURGERIES - 1980

~

Doreen surprised me on my 40th birthday with a handmade, white cable-knit cardigan sweater! It is very beautiful, and I still treasure it. Doreen loved our reunion. She never hesitated to express love for her older sister's firstborn. Doreen's birthday is April 9th, two days after my birthday. On April 9, 1989, I wrote the following to her daughter, Karen:

> I called your mom to thank her for the beautiful sweater she knit me for my 40th birthday and to wish her happy birthday! In the afternoon, John called. Then Grandma Williamson got on the extension. It was a very special call for me. I always wanted her to talk to me when she was ready. We were going to get together in July, but I got sick. I'm sure we'll meet another time.

Emily and I drove from Buffalo in July 1989. We had dinner with Doreen and her family. We planned to see John and Grandma Williamson the next morning and Johnnie Walker in the afternoon.

By the time we got to our hotel in Montreal in the evening, I could feel the onset of a throat infection. About once a year, for many years, I came down with strep, full blown with fever and chills. In the early years, I had to wait for a culture to grow before I could be treated with antibiotics—enough time to become really ill! So, in Montreal, the next morning, I knew I needed to get home. My first meeting with Grandma had to be postponed. She and Frances visited us in Buffalo the next summer.

I also realized that Emily and I needed to bypass Johnnie Walker's farm in Hemmingford, south of Montreal, and go straight home. I had been very excited to meet Johnnie and learn more about Joan and see the farm they both loved.

It still saddens me to recall the missed opportunity to meet with Joan's dear friend. I expected to reschedule our get-together during a future holiday, but it never happened.

I hope to visit Hemmingford before long and meet with people who knew Johnnie and maybe even Joan. I have been in touch with a couple of the local folks. Johnnie lived for thirteen years after Joan's passing. He died April 12, 1996 at the age of 71.

～

On April 21, 1990, I wrote to Doreen and Karen: "I'm thinking of Joan. Tomorrow would be her 61st birthday. So young. Thank you for the picture of her. I know life goes on. I do accept that. But still there is so much I don't know and never will. If you ever think of a particular memory you'd like to share with me, I'd love to hear it."

Doreen and I continue to keep in touch by phone. She turned 88, April 9, 2018. I love our conversations. She is patient with my endless curiosity about the family, always open and honest with me. I have saved all her letters and here is how she closes: "Well Love, I must go as I have a lot to do. Always thinking of you. Love, Doreen."

I know Doreen expected us to visit her more often than we could. I maintained communication with everyone, although less so over time. We eventually settled into a pattern of sending cards at birthdays and holidays.

～

Joan's family always knew about me. They knew Joan was my birthmother. Likewise, Mom and Dad knew Ian was their child; they had conceived him before Dad became gravely ill. Stephie and I were adopted when they wanted more children. We three were "Ian and the girls." But, as much as they loved each of us, did they think differently about Ian, their own flesh and blood, the way Joan's family always thought about me, their flesh and blood?

During a visit to my parents' new home in Vermont, sometime in the late eighties, I discovered the startling answer to my question. Mom and Dad had created a photo wall in the main hallway. Portraits of the two of them were prominently centered and Ian's was centered below them. For a split second, I was confused. "Where are the girls?" I looked over to the right, about four feet and down. There we were! Yes, I get it. Bloodline. But whoever wants to be off to the side on a *public* family photo wall?

I'm reminded how Ville Marie referred to my parents as my adoptive parents, and I'd corrected them. My parents were my *only* parents. I never said "adoptive." However, I was startled to find out that my parents *did* differentiate. Ian shared their bloodline, Stephie and I did not. Therefore, our portraits were off to the side. Adoption is complicated. I wanted to be below my parents on the wall, like Ian. *I also want to find* **my** *bloodline!*

Stephie's and my portraits could have been on either side of Ian. Far right and down was simply too startling for someone who had only explicitly known one set of parents, one brother, and one sister for thirty-eight years.

From 1998 to 2003, both of my families suffered losses. Doreen's husband died in the winter of 1998 during a terrible snowstorm. I remember she told me how difficult it was for family and friends to get to the funeral.

My brother died in April 1999 when his truck skidded off a highway in Wyoming during a spring snowstorm. He was just 54 and left behind my sister-in-law and four beautiful children. For my parents, they lost their only biological child. The grief was almost too much to bear.

In June 2000, my mom's breast cancer returned. She was 80 years old—still doing crossword puzzles until she needed care in the hospice unit at the Kingston Hospital.

John Williamson died from lung cancer in 2000.

The next year, my dad died at age 85. A blood clot formed in his abdomen, and he didn't recover from the emergency surgery. With everything Dad endured after WWII and for the rest of his life, it is amazing that he lived as long as he did.

Grandma Williamson died in January 2003 at the age of 96. Frances had pancreatic cancer and passed away in February 2003.

I was living under a dark cloud of grief.

11

SAVED DOCUMENTS

Joan's brother, John, gave me a number of important documents that have special meaning for me. I remember how he explained each one and I am confident he understood my appreciation for his thoughtfulness and kindness.

I have the original document Joan signed on May 20, 1949, relinquishing me to the Children's Aid Society of Montreal Incorporated. I regret that I never thought to ask John if he had similar documents or information regarding the other babies. Doreen recalls that Joan was required to take care of the baby boy born in 1953 for the first six weeks of his life, as she had done for me, but not for the baby girl born in 1955.

I formally requested that Batshaw contact both of these siblings and provide them with Joan's medical history, as well as medical information on other members of her family, particularly Frances's pancreatic cancer and John's lung cancer.

Joan's fourth baby was born in Ormstown. Joan named her Shirley. Her adoption was private. I hope someday I'll have the opportunity to speak with people at the hospital in Ormstown and ultimately find Shirley. She also deserves to have her maternal medical history.

~

Joan was first diagnosed with breast cancer in 1977. I have the insurance document titled, ATTENDING PHYSICIAN'S STATEMENT OF DECEASED'S DISABILITY PRIOR TO DEATH. Her last day of work was December 20, 1982. She died July 21, 1983. For seven months, she was not well enough to work. That is a long time for someone as diligent and loyal to her workplace as Joan was. She bravely hung on to life.

Diagnosis given—carcinoma R & L breasts. Under remarks:

Mar 30, 1977	L. modified radical mastectomy
Oct. 3, 1978	incisions biopsy R. lymphadenectomy L.
Oct. 10, 1978	R. modified radical mastectomy

The same doctor completed another insurance document: PROOFS OF DEATH—PHYSICIAN'S STATEMENT. Joan went back to work after her surgeries in 1977 and 1978. Then in 1982, the cancer returned. "The interval between onset (return) and death was one year." Cause of death was "carcinoma breasts, metastasized to lung, bone & skin." Two other physicians also treated Joan and an autopsy was performed.

Joan's funeral took place at St Clement's Anglican Church in Verdun on July 25th. This is the church Joan and her family always attended. Her dad was the organist and her mother, an active volunteer. The entire family attended church regularly.

I am sure her family was relieved that her suffering was over. They also told me they took comfort in knowing she was with her dad now. But still, her death was heartbreaking for everyone.

The document from St Clement's Church measures 8 1/2" x 14." It's on heavy cardstock with a bright-red embossed seal. The witnesses listed are J.R. Williamson or John, and her dear friend, John Walker, nickname Johnnie.

Clarke, MacGillivray, White Funeral Directors hosted five visitations: one on Friday, and two on both Saturday and Sunday. The funeral and burial were Monday, July 25th. I have the embossed Burial Certificate, dated July 28. John also gave me a map of The Mount Royal Cemetery. It shows the location of Joan's grave.

Finally, John created a four-page document honoring Joan. He used black calligraphy transfer letters—a difficult task requiring a steady hand and plenty of patience! Between my visits to Verdun, he added my name with *Other Members of the Family* and handed me my own copy.

This document has all the dates and details, from Joan's passing at the Jewish General Hospital to the funeral service and interment at Mount Royal Cemetery. He lists full family names, including Mary Grace Williamson (1944–1945). Birthdates are included for their parents (my grandparents) and the date Grandpa Williamson died.

John was an organized and precise gentleman. He graduated from high school and worked as an electrician. Now more than ever, as I reflect back on my reunion with the Williamson family, I recognize that John made all the crucial and thoughtful decisions to support me and introduce me to the others. He took my phone call in April 1988 when Grandma wasn't ready to talk to me. He could have easily stayed out of it.

I believe that the kindness and support I received from John came from the unconditional love he had for his sister. Not for one second did he express shame for her pregnancies. In fact, he had compassion for her tragic losses. John was her caregiver when she was dying from cancer, even helping her bathe and dress—a loving and devoted brother.

For me, John made sure that the reunion with my birth-mother's family was carefully planned and welcoming. He gave me the family photo and all the documents, but most importantly, he showed me the love he was sure Joan would have given, and then relayed the good news of our reunion to the rest of Joan's family.

I am so grateful, John. I miss you.
Love, Bonnie

12

BIRTHFATHER INQUIRIES

I began searching for my birthparents in May 1983. The non-identifying information came in dribs and drabs, particularly regarding my birthfather. With each inquiry, I was told there was nothing more to tell me. Parent Finders of Montreal was very helpful during this process. Following their suggestions, I'd write back to Ville Marie with further questions, and occasionally receive another tidbit of information!

September 8, 1983: Ville Marie Social Service Centre

I am sorry, but we have no further information on your biological father, except that he lived and worked in Montreal.

December 7, 1983: Ville Marie Social Service Centre

It is not clear in the record whether your biological father was aware of the pregnancy. Your birthmother had not seen him for several months at the time of your birth and thought it unlikely she would ever see him again. Marriage had never been discussed.

March 7, 1984: Ville Marie Social Service Centre

I apologize for the delay in answering your letter of
January 26, 1984, and am sorry to tell you that there
is no information recorded about your birthfather
beyond what has already been given, except that
he was employed as a motor mechanic. This will be
very frustrating for you, but I am afraid that there is
nothing more to tell you.

~

During the next few years, I was busy getting to know Joan's
family. In 1991, I was ready to resume my search for my birthfather. Even though my first search had been for both of my
birthparents, Ville Marie required me to submit a whole new
application, including proof of identity such as ... a birth certificate. How sadly ironic is that?

It was as if they never knew me. My file had been returned
to the basement archives.

In February 1992, they acknowledged receipt of my application, and stated, "When we are able to determine that we
are in possession of dossiers relating to your situation, you
will be informed." And five months later, I was told: "We
have verified that we are in possession of your dossiers and
that you are on the waiting list for Post Adoption Services as
of July 14, 1992." It was a long, form letter about budget cuts
and understaffing. Clearly, Post Adoption Services were their
lowest priority—frustrating, but understandable. "You will be
contacted when your name reaches the top of the waiting list."

In August 1992, only two weeks later, Ville Marie informed
me that they would not reopen my search for my birthfather.
"There would appear to be nothing to be added to the medical
information, which you have already received in the past."

I have no idea why they referred to "Medical Information" as I had not received any medical information. However, the main paragraph explains their policy more clearly than prior communications, and why they were refusing to reopen my search:

> The information you are now seeking concerns your birthfather. At times, the birthfather may be named in our files but not on the birth certificate as is the situation in your case. Under these circumstances, we regretfully are unable to help you. We cannot always be certain that he is aware of the pregnancy or birth, or that the name in the file is accurate, since it was given by the mother, not by the father.

Since 1983, Ville Marie had been giving me non-identifying information about my birthfather. Now in 1992, nine years later, they cast doubt on all this information, because it was given to them by my birthmother. I have always accepted the fact that there was a good chance my birthfather did not know about Joan's pregnancy. However, there is also a good chance he did.

I was told that friends in the neighborhood knew Joan was pregnant. When the family attended church without Joan, people talked. Joan and my birthfather dated, probably for at least a number of weeks. It wouldn't surprise me if Joan never told him she was pregnant, but that he became aware that she was, from chatter in the neighborhood. In any case, the information she gave the social worker suggests to me that she was telling the truth and certainly knew his name. I believe it is disrespectful to imply otherwise.

The rejection I received from Ville Marie in 1992 stopped me in my tracks. I remember feeling that this was it. I was at the end of the road. I thought I would never know my birthfather.

~

I was still communicating regularly with Joan's family, as they were an important part of my life now. On Easter Sunday 1994, I donated an Easter Lily plant at our church, "Given in Memory of Joan Helen Williamson by Bonnie Parsons." Joan's sister, Frances, and her friend, Jean, came to lunch in May 1994. I still have Jean's thank you note.

In 1998, I was ready to search again. An adoptee's need-to-know cannot be denied! I phoned Ville Marie Social Service Centre to reopen the search for my birthfather. I also wanted to be sure that Ville Marie had my permission on file for my half-siblings to contact me if they wanted information.

The social worker was friendly and helpful. I was not required to complete an application this time, much to my relief. That same day, I wrote to the social worker and included background information supporting my requests. For the first time, I wrote my letter on a computer with a hard drive! I printed it out for mailing.

It's important to note that, between each new request for a search for birth family, a number of years would have passed, and I would be communicating with different social workers. For that reason, I included enough personal information to support my case. In addition, I included previous requests and results. My last sentence in July 1998, "I hope this letter provides the information you need as well as a connection to other relevant events."

Mailing to Canada takes six to ten days and requires patience! So, I was shocked to receive a relatively quick response from Batshaw Youth and Family Centres. In 1992, Ville Marie had been renamed Batshaw Youth and Family Centres, in honor of Manny Batshaw, as explained in Chapter 5. Here is the highlight of the response I received:

> In order to find out if the file contained enough information for a search to be done, I did a very thorough review of the dossier. The file does contain his name, which must remain confidential, but it is a common last name and there is no date of birth recorded. In addition, the company for which he worked no longer exists. With such a lack of information, especially without at least an approximate age, a search would be impossible.
>
> ... I am sorry we could not be of more assistance.

I appreciated the *very thorough review of the dossier* and the spirit of kindness expressed in the letter. But, to receive another refusal to search for my birthfather was *very* disappointing!

Unfortunately, I'd never thought to mention in my letter that I thought Joan and my birthfather were about the same age, having met at an outdoor summer dance. His company no longer existed, but how would the social worker know that without having checked it out? Had she started to search for him?

She also stated that it was very possible he hadn't known Joan gave birth to me. Without birth control, a pregnancy at 19 is not surprising. Birth control was not available in Quebec in the late 1940s. Nevertheless, legitimate or illegitimate, I had a right to my identity and my heritage.

Today, the popularity of genealogy on TV and the internet illustrates the fundamental human need to learn about our ancestors and our roots around the globe. Adoptees yearn for the most basic facts to begin a family tree: What was my name and who were my parents?

Clearly, the letter I received gave me new information. His name was in the file, his company no longer existed, and they had continued to see each other during some part of her pregnancy. But the best gift of all was that he had a common last name. I think this may have shortened the social worker's search, because it made a search more difficult. She chose not to go down that rabbit hole! However, I was pleased. It was a new tidbit!

The first letter I received with non-identifying information, in July 1983, stated that my birthfather had an Irish father. In time, *"a common Irish last name"* would prove to be a truly valuable clue, but not any time soon.

The 1998 roadblock shut down my search efforts for a number of years. It came at a time when I was very busy with family and work responsibilities. I do recall considering hiring a private detective. I really was at a loss.

~

Though my focus, at this time, was on finding my birthfather, it would eventually widen to include my half-siblings—Joan's three children born after me. They had a right to know about her breast cancer and other family medical history.

I retired from my full-time employment in 2008. Part-time work and moving kept me preoccupied for the next few years. In the summer of 2013, I was back at it again. Search request number four for my birthfather! As in the past, I began with a phone call to Batshaw Youth and Family Centres. After fifteen years, I was frustrated, but not surprised that they required a whole new application. *They had to verify that they had a file on me!*

My follow-up letter to the phone call stated two requests: First, I wanted to give my permission once again for my maternal half-siblings to contact me. Second, I wanted agency help finding my birthfather. I included my complete application with my letter.

September 16, 2013

Dear Batshaw,

Thank you for taking the time to talk to me. As per our discussion, I would like my address and phone numbers updated in my file. I understand that you cannot search on my behalf for my half-siblings, but if they make an inquiry, I want to be sure that they receive the updated information. Here are the details of the four babies Joan Helen Williamson gave up for adoption [...]

My second request is for help finding my birthfather. I am very concerned, because I believe he is in his mid-eighties. I know his mother was French and his father Irish. He was a motor mechanic, and he has a common Irish name. I believe he lived in the same area as Joan, because they met at an outdoor summer dance in Verdun when Joan was 19.

I would like to meet him and chat, see photos, and obtain medical history. I am enclosing a recent photo. Feel free to share it with my birthfather, his family, or my half-siblings. If he is deceased, I would like to visit with next-of-kin to obtain medical information, etc.

My communication with Ville Marie Social Services Centre dates back to May 1983. Curiosity about my birthparents grew when I became a mom. Joan died of breast cancer in July 1983. Unfortunately, with closed records, I was unable to reunite with her. Five years later, I finally met Joan's family and visited them in Verdun, Saint-Lazare, and Mississauga. I am still in touch with Joan's sister, Doreen, in Saint-Lazare.

From our conversation, I know you have an understanding of adult adoption searches, for which I am grateful. My parents were devoted to me and always supportive. I am retired from thirty-eight years in education.

Finding my birthfather is all about who he is, medical history, appearance, interests. I've wanted to learn about him for years, but it always seemed impossible. I was told, "He probably did not know you had been born; therefore, why would you want to find him?"

I hope you can help. I already truly appreciate the time you gave me when we chatted, and I look forward to hearing from you.

Sincerely,
Bonnie Parsons

It wasn't long before I received confirmation that my application had arrived and that, "We will contact you when we are able to determine that we are in possession of the files relating to your situation." *Oh yes, you have my files!*

~

Four months later, in January 2014, I received a phone call from a social worker, as well as written confirmation that my name was on the waiting list. They had finally decided to search for my birthfather!

Why was a search approved in 2014, but denied in all the previous decades? I was 64. He had to be at least 80 years old! Is this a strategy? There was a good chance he was deceased.

Is there a policy to finally agree after an adult adoptee has requested the search four times, over three decades?

Frustrating, but nevertheless, I was relieved that they agreed to search for me. I wanted to know. It was my heritage and my right to know.

13

SURPRISE AGENCY SUMMARY

In January 2014, Batshaw finally agreed to search for my birthfather. Accompanying that notification was a nine-page *Summary for the Adopted Person*, or *background information report*. On my application, I'd checked "yes" to receive a *summary of my socio-biological background*. Three different titles for the same document. Not surprisingly, I had completely forgotten about it, and I had no idea what it contained! I was a little nervous. Would I find disturbing information? What had they kept from me all these years?

First, I was disappointed that the adoption agency did not acknowledge that, after my five-year search, I had found Joan's name in her obituary in 1988. They knew I had met Joan's family and that we have a loving relationship. Where is the respect for an adoptee who has accurately identified her birthmother against all odds?

I have stated Joan's full name and other identifying information in my letters for years, to Ville Marie and now to Batshaw. Nevertheless, my *surprise summary* had non-identifying information only. And the fact that it was called a "summary" made me wonder once again what they had left out. If the province of Quebec ever opens files for adoptees, I hope to finally see everything and have what belongs to me!

Secondly, most pages in the summary had a number of N/A responses—information not available. I was disappointed to see so many N/A, especially on the birthfather pages. However, I did learn that Joan reported, "She would see him frequently in her community..." This was good news. I was confident that Joan knew his name, even though she had little to report about his family.

I was not surprised that a teenage girl in a relationship with a teenage boy was not familiar with his family! After all, it was 1948, in Verdun, Quebec and Joan's strict religious upbringing was mentioned more than once in the report.

~

The summary included a couple of very significant dates. I try to imagine what each moment was like for Joan and me. I was born on April 7th at forty-weeks gestation, after twenty-seven and a half hours of labor. Had she known what to expect? Was anyone with her? She named me Betty, but I don't know why. It is not a family name that I am aware of. The summary contained the dates of when I was given over to foster care, and when I left it, as well as when the adoption was finalized.

My heart aches for her, knowing that she was required to take care of me for six weeks—and she knew our time together would end. It had to have been heart-wrenching to leave a newborn. On May 20th, six weeks after my birth, Joan handed me over to foster care. I'm weepy for both of us.

The summary described again my birthmother's appearance, hobbies, religious upbringing, and personality. Another section stated, "It was noted in the file that your birthmother resembled her father. Her father was five foot seven, slim build, black hair, and hazel eyes."

The health of the whole family was described as "good." Medical records are very significant for adoptees. Unfortunately, everyone is relatively young in many cases when the information is gathered, and thus it is not as meaningful as records later in life. A turning point for many adoptees, myself included, is pregnancy and/or parenting when medical questions haunt us. It did reference my maternal grandmother's Rh negative blood, though, which I wish I had known when we were ready to start a family.

~

When adoption files are closed, adoptees are unable to contact biological relatives for medical histories. It can be a serious and even life and death situation to treat someone without a medical history. An appeal has to be made in a court of law and even then, there is no guarantee that an adoption file will be opened.

Early in my search, I was told that there had been a fire at the Catherine Booth Hospital, and the hospital records were lost. It was a big disappointment. All I knew was that I weighed 6 lb. 14 oz. *Length, Blood group, cranial circumference, thorax perimeter, and APGAR all say N/A.*

The hospital is still there in Montreal. It is no longer the Catherine Booth Salvation Army Home for unwed mothers. Today it is the Montclair Residence for seniors. I'd like to visit it someday and walk the halls, to be where Joan lived before I was born and where she lived and took care of me for the first six weeks of my life.

~

Section E. *Development of child*

When I was six months old, they noted that I was healthy and like all babies, a cutie!

You were described as a very pretty baby, eyes turning brown, fair hair, and alert. You sat with support, you rolled over, reached and grasped well. You laughed and imitated sounds. You were not immediately responsive with strangers. You stared at them and were very quiet, but you were responsive and happy with the foster family. You were described as well adjusted, a content bright lovable child.

Losing my birthmother at six weeks was the first and most traumatic loss. I then entered the foster care system. I am grateful for the care I received. I would love to meet my foster family if that opportunity ever arose. The agency notes are the only information I have about the family. I believe I was in one foster care home from six weeks of age to almost eight months.

I also think that foster parents have to protect their emotions to some degree and not become too attached to the infants in their care because eventually, in most cases, the babies will be adopted by another family. Can an infant comprehend, on an implicit level, this less-than unconditional love?

When I first read the paragraph about my *development* in foster care, I felt grateful and relieved that I appeared to have settled into my new environment with my foster mother. I had adjusted to life in the foster care system. However, I knew that, just a few months later, I was again faced with traumatic loss. Dad said the foster mother was kind and old compared to him and Mom, probably in her 50s. He remembered nothing else—they were just thrilled to receive their baby daughter!

My parents and I never discussed my transition from foster care to their care. What a huge adjustment it must have been for everyone. Dad was usually not feeling well at the time, Ian was an active three-year-old, and Mom didn't function well when things were chaotic. By all accounts, I was a good sleeper, which had to have helped.

When I was ten months old, the summary notes state: "In February 1950, you were described as very attractive, friendly, and extremely outgoing. You crawled vigorously and were able to pull yourself up on your feet holding onto furniture."

I have no doubt that if Joan had seen me at this young age, she would have felt she'd made the right decision. Her *adoption plan* was to have me placed with a family that could provide a better life for me than she could possibly have provided.

But I can't dismiss the trauma of our separation on May 20, 1949. It was not a superficial event, as proponents of adoption assure unwed mothers, like Joan, and adult adoptees, like me.

～

So much is written now about how relinquishing a baby affects the birthmother. Scientific research explains the neurological changes in a new mother's brain. *The Atlantic* magazine has an informative article by Adrienne LaFrance in their Jan 8, 2015 issue entitled, "What Happens to a Woman's Brain When She Becomes a Mother":

> From joy and attachment to anxiety and protective-ness, mothering behavior begins with biochemical reactions. On the most basic level, these changes, prompted by a flood of hormones during pregnancy and in the postpartum period, help attract a new mother to her baby. In other words, those maternal feelings of overwhelming love, fierce protectiveness, and constant worry begin with reactions in the brain.

The depth of these feelings causes a devastating trauma when the mother and infant are separated. Painfully, the trauma is enduring. My sister cried for years after she relinquished her son. I have read countless similar statements of despair and suicidal thoughts. Shame, loss, and anger are debilitating.

Some women go on to have more children, while many can't reconcile having another after losing their firstborn. Relinquishment causes not only heartbreak but also medical, emotional, and psychological problems. LaFrance states, "Mothers and infants are both hardwired to love and need one another."

Fortunately, it has become more common for unwed mothers to keep their babies. We have seen this shift over the last few decades. Our society is more tolerant and accepting of our differences and individual preferences.

In reality, there are cases where parents and the extended family cannot care for a child. The child may be placed in a foster home, and adoption may be in the best interest of the child. In these cases, every effort needs to be made to reconnect children and families if at all possible. If adoption is necessary, the adoptive parents should be given the record of the child's original identity. Hopefully, the adoption is "open" and there is an agreement about shared communication and visitations. And when the child reaches age 18, the identifying information is turned over to the child.

~

My *Summary for the Adopted Person* has brought me closer to Joan. Even though it is a summary, and I hope to see my file one day, I have been able to piece together its details with the information I received from the agency over the years, as well as treasured details from Joan's family.

I have a better understanding of Joan's relationship with my birthfather now. And I have a clearer picture of my development at different stages as I moved from Joan's care to foster care and finally to my family—three very different circumstances and environments in about twenty-one months!

"And So It Goes" by Billy Joel is playing in my mind.

14

A BATSHAW SEARCH

Ten months went by after hearing that I was finally on the waiting list for a search for my birthfather. On November 17, 2014, Ellen from Post Adoption Services at Batshaw called me. She explained that the person they believed to be my birthfather died four years ago, at the age of 80, in Montreal. His obituary was in the *Montreal Gazette*.

She explained that there were records of a couple of other individuals with similar names, but they had lived in past centuries! For this reason, she believed the gentleman who died four years ago was my birthfather. He initially had perforated gastric ulcers and died from pneumonia and adult respiratory distress syndrome. Ellen then repeated the clue I had heard before: My birthfather had a common Irish last name!

From Ellen's perspective, she and I were done. She said my file was now closed. I should watch for changes regarding access to adoption files in Quebec Bill #47, which was an act to amend the Civil Code and other legislative provisions as regards adoption, parental authority, and disclosure of information.

I heard compassion in her voice. I believe she specializes in post adoption services. She seemed to understand my need to search. *You are looking for your story.* However, I am very sure that Ellen thought this would be our last conversation.

One week later, a letter arrived with the information on my birthfather's death. It was a written confirmation of everything Ellen told me. It was signed by Ellen and stamped and signed by the Commissioner of Oaths. Very official!

In the last paragraph, Ellen again expressed her compassion: "I am sorry that the outcome of your search has resulted in such a disappointing outcome for you and your family. Should you have any questions or concerns, please do not hesitate to contact me at tele #." Ellen and I would have another very important conversation.

Ellen told me that my birthfather died four years ago at the age of 80. That would mean he died around November 17, 2010. She did not give me an exact date, because that would qualify as identifying information, I'm sure. She told me he died in Montreal and that his obituary was in the *Montreal Gazette*. He had a common Irish last name. I did not think twice about my next move. I had enough information to search for his obituary!

~

My first task was to research common Irish surnames. I started with the top ten I found online. Second, I decided to search the obituaries from November 1, 2009—November 30, 2010. I searched each name in each month and found nothing. Then, I expanded my list of common Irish surnames to about twenty-five in all. From the additional names, I still came up empty-handed.

Eventually, it occurred to me that Ellen may have rounded up the date of his death to include December 2010. After all, she said he died four years ago. Was she talking years, rather than actual months or days?

When I searched by name up to December 31, 2010, I found three possibilities. One gentleman, last name Campbell, was from British Columbia, another was a golfer in a Montreal suburb with the last name Kennedy. Finally, I found Ronald Kelly of Montreal, who died December 1, 2010 at the age of 80. He was the only match! His obituary states that he had a common law wife, a brother, age 77, and many children, grandchildren, and great-grandchildren.

Having found the *very common* Irish surname, I turned to ancestry.com and located F. W. Ronald Kelly, who died on December 1, 2010 at the age of 80. It certainly appeared to be the same gentleman. My search angel, Vicki, found Ronald, brother Wesley, and a third brother in a family tree in Ancestry. (More about Vicki in the next chapter.)

I contacted the owner of the tree. She was a first cousin of the three brothers. Wesley died in 2012. J. A. Robert, nicknamed Bobby, suffered from kidney disease and died following two transplant operations in 1966 at the age of 28.

About a week later, the day before Thanksgiving, I called Ellen at Batshaw. I left her a voicemail message and asked that she return my call. At this point, I wanted some kind of verification from her that I had indeed found my birthfather's obituary. Knowing that, by Quebec law, she could not tell me or verify his exact name, I came up with a strategy that would help me if she agreed to it.

It was Thanksgiving Day 2014, and I was preparing our family dinner. My husband and daughter were out running, and I was alone at home. The phone rang, "Happy Thanksgiving!" I said, thinking it must be family or friends.

To my surprise, it was Ellen calling from Montreal. Canadian Thanksgiving is celebrated in October, and she had no idea it was our American Thanksgiving Day. Ellen is a very friendly gal and a good listener. I told her I'd done an online search for my birthfather's obituary in the *Montreal Gazette* archives.

Then I used my strategy: "If I give you a common Irish last name and I am way off base, will you tell me? For example, Murphy?" Immediately, she said, "It's not Murphy." I told her I had found F. W. Ronald Kelly, nicknamed Ronnie. This time, Ellen did not say I was way off base. Wow, I could tell she was surprised and impressed, but she made it very clear that she could not confirm it. She had to *toe the party line*, so to speak! However, she wanted to know every detail about my research methods. I was thrilled! My strategy had worked!

Finally, I told Ellen a couple of heart-warming examples of synchronicity. My husband and I have one son, and his name is Ronald! Coincidently, he is a kidney transplant surgeon. Bobby, Ronald's youngest brother, had two kidney transplant surgeries in the 1960s.

Ellen told me that synchronicity stories like these are not uncommon in adoption. Ellen and I said goodbye. This was our last conversation, until three years later!

∼

I learned more about Bobby's kidney transplants. He had travelled from Montreal to Denver, Colorado for the surgeries. One of the attending doctors in our son's residency knew Bobby's surgeon. Bobby had lived with kidney disease and dialysis treatments for many years. The kidney transplants were the final attempts to save his life. His death at age 28 was devastating to his family and friends, most especially his parents.

I often think of my grandparents. Their only son died during WWII when his airplane went down in a training mission. And my parents lost their only son and biological child when his truck careened off the highway in a snowstorm. When people say that parents are never the same after the death of a child, I believe that is true. After my brother died, my heart ached for my parents more than for myself. I could feel how devastated they were to lose their son.

In the adoption literature, many have written about the loss of an infant being as grievous as the death of a child. However, in relinquishment and closed adoptions, the birthmother has no way of knowing what happened to her baby. There is no end to the sorrow and anxiety of not knowing.

Thanksgiving Day 2014 was a day filled with memories and gratitude. I had searched and found Ronald Kelly's obituary. Ellen at Batshaw came as close as she possibly could under Quebec law to verifying my finding. If his surname was not Kelly, I believe she would have said, "It's not Kelly," just as she had said, "It's not Murphy!" Instead, she was very impressed. Yet, under Quebec law, she could not confirm anything.

Ellen was very kind and thoughtful and genuinely interested in *my story*. Ronald's obituary contained a lot of information, particularly the names of his wife, brother, and children. Now I desperately wanted to see pictures and meet his family.

Joan's family had welcomed me. Her brother, John, gave me a family portrait when we met in Montreal. Joan's sister, Doreen, knit me a sweater for my fortieth birthday! Eventually, I had photos of Joan at all stages of her life.

These were my cherished memories by the time I found Ronald Kelly's obituary. I was not prepared for anything different.

15

ENLIGHTENMENT AND EMPATHY

In the beginning of my search for my biological heritage, there was no internet. Handwritten communications, library research, phonebooks, and the telephone were the tools I used then. I had an old typewriter, but I found it was easier to write letters by hand.

Our lives are very different now. Adoption articles, registries, and accounts of searches and reunions are available online. People are searching. People are hoping to be found! Social media is an excellent source of information and support. In fact, I still find it amazing how much information is there, available at our fingertips, any time of day or night.

After I submitted my fourth request to Batshaw to search for my birthfather, I registered at a Canadian online site. I was hoping to be found by any biological relative. I believed I was simply adding my name to a list, along with other adoptees or birthparents searching for family. However, almost immediately, a search angel picked up my case. Her name is Vicki Hunt, and she's a fellow adoptee from Canada.

Vicki volunteers her time to help folks like me. She is very knowledgeable and savvy. Vicki is my modern-day Candy and Bev at Parent Finders. We have talked on the phone, but most of our communication is online. What a difference the internet makes!

Vicki's first task was to verify my identity. I had to explain the Eleanor Mary/Bonnie and Fairbairn/Parsons names. Within minutes, Vicki sent me the birth names of my maternal half-siblings and their birthdates. She even had the adopted name of the baby boy and was starting to search for him. Unfortunately, his name is very common. *Too many common surnames!*

Vicki and I emailed back and forth, getting to know each other and sharing our experiences as adoptees. We "friended" on Facebook! Soon, I took Vicki's advice and opened a second Facebook account in my original name, Betty Williamson, again in hopes that someone might be searching for me.

Vicki frequently recommended books and articles and gave me many very helpful suggestions. She is always there for me, with same-day responses!

~

The more I reached out and read, the more I felt challenged by my most difficult question: How could Joan have relinquished four infants?

I couldn't shake it! Deep down, I longed to understand her decisions. There had to be an explanation. Joan had so many good qualities. How could I accept that she was uncaring and hard-hearted or that relinquishing her newborns had not been excruciating?

I had a long way to go before I understood. Maybe I was focusing too much on the *how*, and not enough on the *why*. *Why did she have to relinquish me and three others?*

I desperately needed an awakening. It took me a couple of years of study before my heart truly understood Joan's heartbreaking and tragic life. My search for Joan led me far beyond her gravesite at The Mount Royal Cemetery in Montreal. I needed to find the answer. How or why could Joan relinquish four infants?

I read about the history of adoption practices in other countries and the need for communities to support unwed mothers and infants. As I mentioned in Chapter 10, I read *Philomena: A Mother, Her Son, and a Fifty-Year Search* and watched the movie several times. Philomena Lee gave birth in an Irish convent for unwed mothers. She lived there with her son until, as a toddler, he was sold to an American couple. Philomena's story is a story of love and sorrow and never forgetting. It was difficult to read and more difficult to watch.

The more I read about adoption, the more I learned about birthmothers, like Philomena, and their infants. I read about the immense suffering experienced by birthmothers. Their pain and sorrow when an infant is relinquished causes unspeakable heartbreak. One's life is changed forever. *I was beginning to understand this.*

Joan wasn't a bad girl. In fact, she was kind, helpful, and generous. She was a hard worker and had the best attendance record in her work place. She was, however, poorly educated. Her home was very strict. Her community believed pregnancy out of wedlock was a sin.

I believe Joan did the best she could in very tough circumstances. The support she needed to raise a child was not there for her. She had brought shame to her family and the only solution was adoption. The heartache with each baby had to have been almost too much to bear. Joan needed education, healthcare, birth-control options, family, and community support.

~

One of my greatest sources of enlightenment is the internet blog, *[birthmother] First Mother Forum (FMF)*. A co-author of the blog, Lorraine Dusky, has written two books about adoption: *Birthmark* and *hole in my heart*. Lorraine lives in Sag Harbor, Long Island, New York, only a short distance from where we lived in 2015. Lorraine writes about becoming pregnant in the 1960s, relinquishing her daughter for adoption, and finding her fifteen years later.

My husband and I attended a book talk on *hole in my heart* that was given by Lorraine at her town library in Sag Harbor. We sat in the front row. There I was, an adoptee at a public event all about adoption! My adoption had always been a personal and somewhat private matter. I became nervous—of course—and had to scratch the tip of my itchy nose throughout her entire talk. The only other time I get an itchy nose is when I'm at the dentist. Fortunately, I was not asked to leave! In fact, we joined everyone for tea afterwards at Lorraine's house.

My story was now much greater than my search for my birthparents. Lorraine's talk was an enlightening event for me. I began to see adoption differently. People refer to the Adoption Triangle—adoptee, adoptive parents, and birthmother. My own experiences had revolved around my adoption and my adoptive family, or *my family*, and very little around my birthmother. Now I needed to hear from birthmothers to understand their experiences and challenges. This became the key to my enlightenment about Joan's decisions. Other birthmothers helped me understand, not only Joan's decisions, but her suffering as well.

I read the *FMF* blog every day and heard the voices of birthmothers in their comments. I finally understood with all my heart that pregnant, unwed women need to be offered help by their families and the community, not shamed. Adoption will sometimes be necessary, but it should be a last option, not the only option.

Hole in my heart tells Lorraine's story as a birthmother. It is also very informative about adoption issues and the need for laws that make original birth certificates and birth records available to adult adoptees upon request.

I kept thinking about my sister and how wrong it was for women to be pressured into giving up their children. I have learned about the pain and sorrow mothers experience with the relinquishment of an infant. I need to let my sister know that I now have a more enlightened understanding.

I wrote to Lorraine regarding my feelings for my sister and my conversation with her:

Hi Lorraine,

I wanted to share something with you. My sister, Stephanie, and I were adopted in Montreal from different families. In our high school years, our family moved to Massachusetts. Stephanie got pregnant in 1967. When it became clear that a marriage was not going to happen, our parents sent her away. She lived with and did housework for a family in a suburb of Boston, Massachusetts. Her son was born in the summer of 1968. Mom and I drove to Boston to see her and the baby. I have never forgotten—he was the only baby awake in the nursery and he had such bright beautiful eyes. Stephanie held him for the few days they were in the hospital and then had to give him up. You know her suffering.

I could see her suffering. I should say, too, that she had a very tough early childhood and wasn't adopted by our parents until she was almost five. Stephanie went on to marry and have another beautiful son and now grandchildren.

As you know, my work on a memoir about my search for my birth family has led to my greater enlightenment about first mothers. My birthmother, Joan, relinquished four babies. I now recognize how tragic it had to have been for her. I've always felt my heart was with my sister, but now I have a much greater understanding of what she endured and how wrong it was for her to be forced to give up her first son. I told my family at Thanksgiving that I wanted Stephanie to know what I have learned.

Today I got that opportunity when I called for her son's address for a Christmas card. She kept chopping nuts for the candies she was making for a cookie swap—I think the phone was next to the cutting board, but I did my best to hang in there. We were going to hang up and chat later so that she could finish the chocolate turtles, but we kept on chatting. She talked about the bitterness she still has toward our parents, how naive she was in retrospect, and how devastating her grief was. She also talked a lot about her first son.

I told her about First Mother Forum and your books and meeting you at your book talk. I explained that my memoir was not just about my search anymore. I told her how terrible I feel about everything she's been through. I sent her the link to your blog. Stephanie is a great reader, and I know she will want to read *hole in my heart*.

Thank you for helping me see the bigger picture. I love the blog and I follow it daily!

～

I desperately wanted to understand why Joan relinquished four babies. During my writing break, I listened carefully and read many accounts from birthmothers. Gradually, my empathy for her suffering led to an enlightenment—Joan *had* to relinquish her babies. She had no choice. There weren't viable alternatives to adoption at that time. She had no support from her family or community. Without support, she had to make the heart-wrenching decisions.

Here is my love note to my birthmother:

Dear Joan,

I understand your decisions. Please do not feel ashamed—you did your best. I am so sorry for all your suffering.

I love you,
Betty aka Bonnie

16

ANCESTRY, DNA, AND A FIRST COUSIN

I have two family trees on ancestry.com. First, I developed my Parsons family tree, beginning with information from my uncle's handwritten family tree. My grand-nieces and nephews can visit the gravestone of their eleven-times-great-grandfather in Scotland from the early sixteenth century!

Then, I created the Williamson Family Tree with everything I knew about Joan's family, going back four generations. Learning one's way around ancestry.com takes patience and time, usually way more time than I'd planned on spending.

DNA testing has become increasingly popular in the last few years. People enjoy working on their family trees and researching the generations that came before them. Now we can connect with each other around the globe instantaneously and easily link the present to the past.

DNA is also used to find family members. Adoptees, birthparents, entire families, search angels, and detectives are all using DNA to find people. The television series *Long Lost Family* uses public records and DNA technology to search for and reunite individuals with their birthparents, children, or biological families.

The Facebook group, *DNA Detectives,* helps members interpret DNA findings. I read posts every day and learn from members' questions and the responses from other members and volunteer administrators. They post DNA charts and tables and refer to articles and other sites that explain DNA findings, and they even offer courses for rookie genealogists!

~

But what do you do when no one agrees to take a DNA test? One day in December 2016, I sought the opinion of my friends in Facebook *DNA Detectives.* I was obviously frustrated and turned to them. I uploaded a photo of Ronald Kelly and one of myself next to it. Here is what I posted with our photos.

> The biggest message I get every day from this group is to never give up. We all deserve to know our heritage, our original names, and information in "our files!" I'm having difficulty convincing anyone in my supposed birthfather's family to get their DNA tested so that I can be absolutely sure it is him. So, until I have DNA results, do you see a resemblance? What do you think? Thanks for taking a moment.

I received thirty-one likes and eleven kind comments. They renewed my hope that I had my guy!

I spent many, many hours on ancestry.com. My closest match, outside of my immediate family, was a third cousin on my birthfather's side. We tried to identify our common ancestor without any luck to date. I matched with a couple of other third cousins, also on my birthfather's side.

Then, I learned about GEDmatch—a free website for people who have already tested at AncestryDNA, 23andMe, Family Tree DNA, or MyHeritage DNA. According to fileinfo.com, "A

GED file is a data file that stores family history and genealogical event data in the standard GEDCOM genealogy format." GEDmatch is a huge database of DNA results. It was surprisingly easy to upload my AncestryDNA to GEDmatch, and my results are now listed among thousands of matches from the other sites.

GEDmatch has a number of tools for delving further into one's DNA results. It also provides an email address for each person. New matches appear in bright green, which fades away after thirty days.

I have made friends through ancestry.com. We try to help out each other. One of my friends recommended that I have my DNA tested with 23andMe and Family Tree DNA. She said that I might find matches that didn't test with AncestryDNA. And not everyone uploads to GEDmatch.

What a great suggestion! AncestryDNA testing has only been offered in Canada in the last couple of years, and I have more Canadians than Americans in my family tree. I thought about it for a few weeks because the tests are expensive. But eventually, I sent away for both kits, hopeful for new, close matches.

23andMe showed a second-cousin match, my closest match yet! She and I emailed and shared great-grandparent names, but we have not found closer common ancestors—yet. Interestingly, she has ancestors on both sides of her family with the same last name, as do I—the same name! She is from Marathon, Ontario on Lake Superior—a beautiful area. She told me that the Group of Seven Canadian painters painted many of their scenes from Marathon. My parents and Joan's family both had paintings by the Group of Seven in their homes. I wish she would upload to GEDmatch.

～

Then I got my results from Family Tree DNA (FTDNA). I was thrilled to see a high match at the top of the list—my first high match outside of my family. It said, "First Cousin, Half-Siblings, Grandparent/Grandchild, Aunt/Uncle, or Niece/Nephew." His name is Marc, and he lives in Ottawa, Ontario. He didn't test with AncestryDNA and has not uploaded to GEDmatch. My ancestry friend was right! Indeed, I needed to dip my toe into each pond, as she suggested!

I emailed Marc with the FTDNA match, but he did not reply to my email for a couple of weeks. Turns out, it was an old email address he rarely used anymore. He had his DNA tested six years ago and had given up checking it because he never had a close match.

As I waited and prayed for a response from Marc, I posted a new question to Facebook *DNA Detectives*. I gave the details about our shared DNA from FTDNA and asked how Marc and I were related. The consensus was first cousins on our fathers' side. There was an outside possibility that we were half-siblings, but more likely, we were paternal first cousins. *Very, very exciting!*

Marc got back to me:
"Hi Bonnie, WOW, if this is true that would be great! Please call me or I can call you. Thanks again."

Marc was adopted in Montreal and raised in Welland, Ontario in a French-speaking family. His English is very good. I was surprised to find out that French was his first language. I was so pleased that we could communicate easily. We talked and laughed for a long time. We have shared family photos.

Marc and I are still trying to solve the mystery of his birth-father—and verify mine! Also, he is waiting for his ancestry. ca (Canada) results. Then he will upload his results from

AncestryDNA and FTDNA to GEDmatch and hopefully find more high matches. *Searching is a slow process.* But at least now, we have each other's support. We share the belief that we have a right to our biological heritage! We don't want to intrude on families we do not know or upset anyone. As Marc says, "...we're looking for our roots and maybe to build a friendship."

~

Before I had DNA results, I focused my time and energy on family trees and searches in ancestry.com. When you start to search for someone, the program asks for information such as name, birthday, locations, and family members. Then it gives you lists of census data, births, marriages, and deaths, with the closest matches at the top of the results. Oftentimes, I have to remove some of the data I included at the beginning of the search in order to get matches. It is ironic that too much information can get in the way!

When you do find something that looks like it matches your ancestor, the site allows you to save it to that person in your tree. You can add anecdotes and photographs, and pretty soon, your tree tells the story of your ancestry. You can also invite guests to view your tree. If you share ancestors, you can each expand your trees.

~

There are also many very useful sites with amazing data. I have used Findmypast, Fold3, Newspapers, Library and Archives Canada, London Metropolitan Archives, and Scotland's People. In Chapter 2, I described the deaths of my mother's first husband and her brother during WWII from newspaper accounts I found online. In the Canadian Archives, *Soldiers of the First World War: 1914–1918*, I found my grandfather's entire service record! Eventually my dad's service record should be available. He has not yet been deceased long enough for his records to be posted. These are public records. I wonder what Dad's will include regarding his scientific work.

Family trees and DNA testing provide different types of information. The downside of family trees is that mistakes can go unchecked. The obvious downside of DNA testing is that it only includes results from those who purchase the kits and send the saliva or cheek swabs back to be tested—obvious, but frustrating.

Many of the DNA testing companies run sales during the holiday season. And many of us who have already tested are hoping to receive more matches in a month or so.

One of the Batshaw adoption caseworkers told me that they use ancestry.com all the time when they are searching for adult adoptees and birthparents.

Marc's results showed up in AncestryDNA in February 2017. There was his name, right below my daughter's—first cousin! He uploaded the results to GEDmatch, and again, he is right under Emily. This is the additional proof we'd hoped for to truly believe we are first cousins. As fellow adoptees, we are in this search together, and close matches mean the world to us!

17

A DNA OFFER!

After I found Ronald Kelly's obituary, my search angel, Vicki, helped me find a gal in ancestry.com who has a "Ronald Kelly" in her family tree. Her name is Lillian. She answered my email and said that she was Ronald's first cousin. Their mothers were sisters. She said, "Would love to hear back from you," and gave me her phone number. I was thrilled!

Five days later, Lillian called me! We had a wonderful talk. She gave me a lot of information about the Kelly family, including relatives and close friends in Montreal.

As I described in Chapter 14, the youngest brother, Bobby, died in 1966 from kidney disease after two failed transplants. Lillian said she believed that Ronald Kelly was my birthfather. "You have received two signs from God that Ronald Kelly is your birthfather: You named your son, Ronald, and he is a kidney transplant surgeon."

Lillian recommended I talk to a woman in Montreal who knew the family well. Lillian called her and got the go-ahead for me to make the call.

About a week later, Lillian emailed me about my phone call and I replied:

Hi Lillian,

We had a wonderful chat. Thank you for making it possible!

We covered a lot of territory, and she was most patient with me as I tried to keep it all straight. I am so grateful for her thoughtful kindness. Like you, she believes I have a right to know who my birth parents were, medical records, etc.

My favorite part was her description of Ronald's personality—extremely kind, generous, hard-working, caring, witty, loved music and having fun. Very sociable and got along well with others.

Lillian, I can't thank you enough for helping me. You are the best!! Bonnie

Lillian was happy for me and asked to be kept informed.

~

I kept going back to my conversation with Ellen from the adoption agency in Montreal. If only she could have simply stated whether or not I had found my birthfather's obituary. She hadn't discounted the Kelly surname, but she stopped short of confirming it for me. I understand that by law, she cannot confirm identifying information.

I decided to get back to Lillian.

January 21, 2015

Dear Lillian,

How are you? I hope you enjoyed the photos of our grandkids. I also hope your holidays were fun and not too stressful. January is flying by.

My latest involvement with ancestry is their DNA program. I sent them my saliva sample and hope to hear back later in February. My family is as curious as I am to see my genealogy. I do not expect any specifics, but you never know.

Please take care. I look forward to hearing from you. Bonnie

"Bonnie, Sorry I have not been in touch. I have not felt well. I was in emergency on Christmas Eve. Yes, I do feel Ronald Kelly is your birthfather. Too bad we didn't know sooner.

Your grandkids are beautiful—I love their Christmas pjs." Lillian

Lillian and I continued to correspond and talk occasionally. In February, we discussed AncestryDNA. Soon after, I suspected she had a change of heart. She wanted me to send her the sequence of events that led me to her ancestry.com site.

Lillian, Here is the sequence that led me to your site:

*11/17/2014 - The Montreal adoption agency (official provincial government) finally searched for my birth-father at my request after decades and found that he died in 2010. They told me he had a very common Irish surname, which they could not tell me.

*I researched common Irish surnames. This took about two days. I found Ronald Kelly's obituary in the *Montreal Gazette* archives.

*My adoption angel started looking in Ancestry and found references to Ronald Kelly on your site. I wrote

to you through Ancestry and you confirmed for me that Ronald was your first cousin.

*11/27/2014 - The agency returned my call from the previous day. She told me she would tell me if I was off base with a name. I told her that I'd found Ronald Kelly's obituary. She was very impressed and asked about my research and strategies. Turns out, I was not off base. I told her I have one son named Ronald!

Thanks again for your support. It means the world to me. Bonnie

I still didn't have a photo of the man described by Batshaw after their search for my birthfather. Months earlier, Vicki suggested I call the funeral home and ask if they had a photo of Ronald Kelly. I thought, *What a great idea!* It was a while before I got up the nerve to make the call, as much as I desperately wanted a photo. Adoptee jitters!

Finally, I called the funeral home. The gentleman was very polite and obliging. I explained that I was working on the Kelly Family Tree. He checked his file and said that he had a photo. I gave him my email address, and he was pleased to send it to me right away! I was very excited, very nervous, and very excited!

As soon as it arrived, I printed it on glossy photo paper and displayed it on my desk. My first thought was, *I've got his nose!* And he has a great smile. I shared it with my family and the closed group *DNA Detectives* on Facebook, as described in the previous chapter. Everyone saw the resemblance.

Vicki saw it and closed my case. *Birthfather Found!*

March 1, 2015

Hi Lillian,

How are you? I hope you had a great weekend.

I finally have a photo of Ronald Kelly. My first thought was that I have his nose! Then his smile, and it went from there. He was probably only about ten years older in the photo than I am today. I am very happy to have this. And I am so hopeful to see other photos taken at different times in his life.

Between you and me, I had this thought yesterday: Yes, Ronnie and Joan acted irresponsibly, but they gave me life and I have children and grandchildren. Now that I have seen photos of both my birthparents, I am prouder than ever of my heritage. And I am profoundly grateful for Ronnie and Joan. I am grateful for all my parents, birth parents and my mom and dad.

I look forward to hearing from you.

Thanks so much for everything! Bonnie

March 8, 2015

Hi Lillian,

Just checking in. We visited with our son Ron today. I showed him the photo of Ronnie Kelly. He saw many similarities between him and me.

Do you think I should reach out to other relatives for more photos? I'm pretty harmless, and Ronnie wasn't married to anyone when I was conceived. So, he didn't "cheat" on anyone. He was just a kid. What do you think? Bonnie

~

In June, Lillian moved over to the dark side. She thought I should get my son to recommend a psychologist, because wanting to find my birth family was crazy!

She thought I should be grateful for my adoption, because she figured I was better off than I would have been with the Williamson and Kelly families. My family had given me a better education! Her tone was crass and nasty.

A week later, I wrote to Lillian. I explained how I had wanted to go to college and to be a teacher. I believe I reached my goals because of my own determination and hard work. Successful people come from all backgrounds. Unsuccessful people do as well.

I wasn't angry at Lillian. I didn't even see it as a setback. Lillian knew more about her family than I did. Unfortunately, in her eyes, I was upsetting the apple cart.

Vicki came through for me, as she always does:

> I read your response to Lillian and was proud of your restraint and integrity. You are "a classy lady." It always makes me angry when other people who could make our lives easier by co-operating and answering our questions truthfully, turn on us, or decide to withhold information. Everyone is entitled to know where they came from ... to know their genealogy and their medical background at a minimum. It is a civil rights issue, pure and simple ... a right which most adoptees are denied. What you ask for is not unreasonable ... remind yourself of this. Obviously, the experience of searching has made you a strong person.

> Someone once told me, "It is the brave ones who look, as they are always the ones capable of dealing with what they find." I think I believe that. I have a small painting that I look at every morning. It says, "Your very

complicated, messy life story matters, tell it." Tell your story, Bonnie. I look forward to reading every word. Best regards always, Vicki

I realized now that I was facing an entirely different reception from the open arms and warm welcome I received from Joan's family. On the other hand, I had my photo! Maybe in the future I'd have more photos and meet a half-sibling or two.

Reunion relationships are fragile. It's easy to move too quickly only to find out you're going backwards. My strategy had been to go slowly and gently. It did not, however, work as well as I'd hoped with Lillian. She was friendly at first, but then acknowledging me became too difficult. Photos and a few pleasant conversations were all I ever asked for. Maybe a "friend" or two on Facebook!

~

Six months later, in November, I sent my letter again to Lillian. Finally, by May 2016, I had a feeling that she might have a different, more positive opinion of me. Just a hunch. So, I gave her a call. We had a good talk. In my notes, I wrote, "Pleasant!" She talked a lot about her family, especially her granddaughter, and she asked about my family.

Then she said that she hoped I was okay with what she'd said in our last conversation when she was nasty. It was sort of an apology, "It's just the way I am," she said. She wanted the telephone number of the Montreal family friend. I was amused that she was asking for the number she had once given to me! I have no idea if she called her. But it gave me a reason to send her an email. I also sent photos of the kids, and the photo I got from the funeral home of Ronald Kelly.

She wrote back:

"Hi, Loved all the pictures! I like the picture of Ron Kelly—kind face. I do believe Ron was very kind and family was important. When I get back on ancestry, I will let you know." Lillian

Lillian recognized Ronald Kelly! This was a red-letter day! The information from Ellen at the adoption agency matched the obituary I found searching for my birthfather. The obituary and the photo were a match! I was one step closer!

Hi Lillian,

Glad you loved the pictures!

Kindness is so important. It was the most important trait I looked for in my students. I believe Ronald Kelly and I would have hit it off—cheerful, funny, loved family, thoughtful, and kind!

Have fun on ancestry! Bonnie

~

Lillian and I had one more challenge. She shocked me one morning with a phone call. We had discussed my DNA results from AncestryDNA. Lillian called to say she wasn't well and wanted to get her DNA tested for me before it was too late. I knew she often didn't feel well, but now, I was stunned. Her only request was that, if it came back without a match, she didn't want me to be upset. I assured her I would be okay.

I was worried about Lillian's health. It sounded like she thought her days were numbered. I called the support team at AncestryDNA for advice. Lillian lives in Ontario, Canada. Basically, she agreed to send in her saliva and asked that I take care of all the details.

AncestryDNA overnighted the kit to me. I registered it online and mailed it to Lillian immediately. In a few days, she felt well enough to produce her sample and take it to the post office. We both expected the results to show a "first cousin once removed match." We believed she and Ronald were first cousins and I was one generation removed.

After about six weeks, the results came to my email: No match! I wasn't exactly upset, but I was very disappointed when the results showed no shared DNA. *None at all!*

Lillian was disappointed that AncestryDNA had embedded her Scottish ancestry into her UK ancestry. She wanted it separated out, because both her parents were Scottish. I understood her frustration and sought an explanation from AncestryDNA. "Lillian, I called AncestryDNA. They had no answer as to why your UK is not broken down. The representative did say they were trying to provide more precise results for people. Disappointing, I know."

Vicki suggested I write to CeCe at Facebook *DNA Detectives*. CeCe stated what I knew to be true: If Lillian and Ronald's biological mothers were sisters and Lillian and I didn't match, then Ronald was not my birthfather. She asked if I had uploaded Lillian's results to GEDmatch. I had, and we did not match there either.

Lillian and I never talked about the fact that our DNA did not match. She did not seem surprised and didn't ask me if I was upset. I still thought Ronald Kelly was my birthfather, and I think Lillian did too. However, the element of doubt remained. I just couldn't shake it!

In October, I reached out to Lillian and asked her if she had ever heard of a gentleman by the name of Marc. At this point, I was anxiously waiting to hear from Marc. Lillian said that she had never heard of him. Within a couple of days, Marc answered my email. In the following note, I relayed this news to Lillian.

11/30/16

Hi Lillian,

I hope you are feeling well. Please let me know.

I have interesting news about Marc, my newfound cousin. He had his DNA tested by Family Tree DNA (FTDNA) about six years ago and received no significant results until I had mine done recently through FTDNA. He was born in Montreal in 1960 and was adopted.

The DNA shows that he and I are first cousins on our birthfathers' side. The DNA results are strong. He has found his birthmother, and she is still alive but suffers from Alzheimer's. Hopefully, she will be able to tell him the name of his birthfather when he visits her.

Marc is very friendly and funny. We have chatted a couple of times.

I have not made any progress on yours and my DNA results. Perhaps there were babies born out of wedlock or adoptions we don't know about. The more people have their DNA tested, the more we will know. I follow an online group called *DNA Detectives*. It has over 30,000 members and everyday matches are made because of DNA testing.

I hope your daughter and granddaughter are doing well. Bonnie

In December, Lillian and I exchanged short emails—nothing relating to my DNA match with Marc. At Christmastime, she was still not feeling well and needed to have more tests done.

We wished each other Merry Christmas!

In March, I wrote to Lillian with updates.

March 6, 2017

Hi Lillian,

Marc and I match in FamilyTreeDNA as well as AncestryDNA—our DNA numbers indicate we are first cousins on our fathers' side. The numbers are not high enough for us to be half-siblings. But they strongly show us as first cousins. Is it possible that his birthfather was Bobby?

I hope you are feeling well. Please take care. Bonnie

To date, I have not heard back from Lillian.

~

On two occasions, Marc had readings with a medium. In both of his readings by different mediums, he was told that a spirit named Bob or Bobby claimed to have been watching over Marc since he was a child. Could it be Bobby Kelly? I shared with Marc how Joan had broken into my session with Rose at Lily Dale.

18

LONDON FOUNDLING HOSPITAL

J oan's mother, Grandma Williamson, was born in Colwyn Bay, Denbighshire, Wales in 1906. Her name was Frances Helen Thurnall (1906–2003). Her parents were Helen Louisa Gulliver (1869–1938) and James Thurnall (1870–1947). That is all I knew about them—until one memorable day when I fell into the rabbit hole, otherwise known as ancestry.com.

Developing a family tree on my birthmother's side was fun! There was no doubt that Joan Helen Williamson was my birthmother! I enjoyed researching my ancestors, and confidently placed each new discovery in the tree.

~

So, my story continues on Joan's side, on my Williamson family tree. I was curious about James Thurnall, my great-grandfather, Joan's grandfather and Grandma Williamson's father. I knew about the other three maternal great-grandparents, but I had no information on James Thurnall. I entered his name into an ancestry.com search and finally found something! His name appeared in the *1881 England Census* in a class list from when he was about 10 years old. In a split second, I had found my great-grandfather. Compared to my search strategies thirty years ago, the internet is magical!

Having been in education my entire career, I was especially curious about this new find. There were twenty-five "scholars" on the class list, between the ages of 10 and 12. James was the youngest. I noted that none of the "scholars" had middle initials or middle names.

At the top of the list, it said, *"London St Pancras Grays Inn Lane, The Hospital for the Maintenance and Education."* I learned that St Pancras was the civil parish, Grays Inn Lane was the district, and The Hospital for the Maintenance and Education was the name of the institution: *The London Foundling Hospital!*

I soon learned that my great-grandfather, James Thurnall, lived in the London Foundling Hospital (LFH) when he was 10 years old. Now I was truly beginning to feel like Alice tumbling down the rabbit hole! What exactly is a foundling hospital, and are foundlings different from adoptees? In both cases, an infant is abandoned by his or her parent and raised by others.

I went from foster care to my adoptive family. I realized that James was raised by the London Foundling Hospital. Both James and I were given new names after our mothers relinquished us. I wanted to learn about James Thurnall's early life. I began to read everything I could find about the LFH.

If I had known about him sooner, I am sure Grandma Williamson would have shared stories about his life with me. She was his only child, and I believe they had a close father-daughter relationship.

~

From my research, I learned that all the records from the Foundling Hospital Archives are kept at the London

Metropolitan Archives (LMA). My next step was to ask for their help:

London Metropolitan Archives:

Please give me direction. I am searching for my great-grandfather, James Thurnall. He is in a class list—at the age of 10 in 1881—at The Hospital for the Maintenance and Education, Grays Inn Lane in St Pancras.

I have had no success searching for a record of his birth or his parents. I'd like to know when he entered the Foundling Hospital and when he left. From what I have read, careful records were kept. As a young man, he went to Wales, where he met and married my great-grand-mother, Helen Louisa Gulliver, in 1903.

Thank you for your assistance. I look forward to continuing my search.

Sincerely,
Bonnie Parsons

The search options from LMA were very helpful. Here is the response I received:

4/19/16

London Metropolitan Archives

Dear Ms. Parsons

Thank you for your recent email.

Records from the Foundling Hospital have been deposited here at London Metropolitan Archives.

An information leaflet entitled Finding Your Foundling is available online.

You are most welcome to visit this office. Details of our opening hours, location, and History Card registration are available on our website: www.cityofLondon.gov.uk/lma.

If you are unable to undertake this work yourself, you may wish to use our Paid Document Research Service. This provides for a paid search by our staff, using the sources available here. You will find more information on our website and an application form is attached, if you would like to use the service.

Yours Sincerely,
CG on behalf of London Metropolitan Archives

The information leaflet, "Finding Your Foundling," describes how the foundlings were cared for and lists the sources at the LMA, bibliography, and web links. Everything is well organized!

The 'System' for care of foundlings was as follows:

- *Admission:*

    Children under 12 months were admitted subject to regulations set down by the General Committee.

    The mother had to present a petition explaining the background; these were not always accepted.

    Once admitted, the children were baptised and renamed, each being identified by an admission number and often a token left by the mother.

- *Nursing:*

    The children were dispatched to wet or dry nurses in the Country. These nurses were mostly in the Home Counties but could be as far away as West Yorkshire or Shropshire.

    The nurses were monitored by voluntary Inspectors.

- *School:*

    Once the children had reached the age of between 3 and 5 they were returned to London to the Foundling Hospital.

    Apart from reading classes, there were practical tasks, music classes, and sewing projects.

- *Apprenticeship:*

    Children were apprenticed to trades or services, or enlisted to serve in the armed forces (especially later on in the nineteenth century, when the hospital's musical tradition was well known).

Not being able to easily visit London, I was thrilled the LMA offered "Paid Document Research Service." The paperwork was a relatively easy process. I printed the "application for search" form, filled it out, scanned it, and sent it back. I didn't have a clue how long it would take them to find documents on James Thurnall. I paid for *up to two hours of work*. It came to $201.00 in American dollars.

They asked for the following information to guide their search. This is everything I submitted:

May 31, 2016

JAMES THURNALL is my great-grandfather.

DOB: 1870 London; DOD: 1947 Denbighshire, Wales

I am very interested in learning about JAMES THURNALL.

This is all I have found out about his early years:

JAMES THURNALL, scholar, is on a class list in 1881 when he was about age 10 at "The Hospital Guilford St Russell Sq London"; 1881 England Census for James Thurnall "London St Pancras Grays Inn Lane the Hospital for the Maintenance and Education."

Can you tell me the circumstances that led up to his residence at the foundling hospital?

Mother's name? Father's name? Siblings?

When did he arrive at the hospital? Who brought him there?

How long did he stay? What was life like?

What records were kept?

Do the records include a photo?

Thank you very much,
Bonnie Parsons

I also included:

Records regarding James Thurnall:

James married HELEN LOUISA GULLIVER in 1903.

Their only child was FRANCES HELEN THURNALL, my grandmother.

Frances married JOHN PASCOE WILLIAMSON in 1928 and their oldest child was my mother, JOAN HELEN WILLIAMSON.

~

I was *very* excited. From an 1881 class list, I had only the name of a 10-year-old boy. I couldn't wait to see what, if anything, they would find. Only two weeks later, a large envelope arrived from London, England! They needed only one hour to search their records and archives for information on James Thurnall, number 21375. The records revealed his date of birth, date of admission to the LFH, baptism, renaming, and apprentice-ship at the age of 14.

I was overwhelmed by what I received—copies of original documents from 1870! They are stunning, and have been saved all these years, almost a hundred and fifty years. They tell a story I could never have imagined. CG explained the LMA search process in the following cover letter. She is now my newest search angel.

In the archives, they located James's mother's petition to have him admitted to the LFH. They sent me a copy of the entire petition! By the time James was relinquished by his mother, he was almost 4 months old. James's mother and Joan Williamson faced similar circumstances in which they were unable to care for an infant. James's mother did what she had to do to give them both a chance at life. She showed courage and love in heart-breaking circumstances.

This search has led me to my great-grandfather, James Thurnall. But I am also learning about his mother, my second great-grandmother, and her family. The more I learn, the more I feel connected to my ancestors. My illusive family tree is now taking shape. Adoptees and foundlings as well as future generations have every right to know the heritage and circum-stances of their ancestors' births.

Dear Ms Parsons

Subject: PDRS (2 hours)

We began our search of the records of the Foundling Hospital by checking the 1851 - 1891 Register of Apprentices (microfilm reference X041/005B). This revealed that James Thurnall (number 21375) was apprenticed on 29th October 1884 to James Davies, a hairdresser, of High Street, Harrow. A copy of the entry is enclosed.

We then checked the General Registers (Microfilm number X041/004) and discovered that his birth was recorded as 6th May 1870 and that he was admitted to the Foundling Hospital on 29th August 1870.

The Baptism Register (Document reference: A/FH/A/14/004/002) recorded that he was also baptised and renamed as James Thurnall on 29th August 1870.

We then located the Petition submitted by his mother. The Foundling Hospital would only care for illegitimate children their mother made a sufficiently strong case for her ability to make a new start in life. Document reference A/FH/A/08/001/002/079 records such a case being made for Mary Anne Wingfield. She is presented as an unmarried 17 year old former servant, who has been abandoned by the father of her child. Her address is given as 1 Nell Gwynne Cottages, Grosvenor Row in Pimlico. The Petition contains some useful information about her and we have enclosed a complete copy.

You have been charged £66.67 for one hour of research. Please do not hesitate to contact us if you have any further questions.

Yours sincerely

The following image shows the cover of the bundle for *The Petition of Mary Anne Wingfield*. The original was folded in fourths and tied up with twine. The statements of support and the actual petition took place in August 1870.

The London Foundling Hospital was founded in 1739 by Thomas Coram. It evolved over the years as times changed. It was, however, always attentive to disease control and the overall health of the children. Its primary purpose remained the same: caring for and educating deserted children.

The instructions in the next document spell out exactly who was eligible to be admitted to the LFH and the process that had to be followed for admission to be considered.

245

Secretary's Office

Foundling Hospital. 8ᵗʰ August 1870

INSTRUCTIONS

To the Mothers of such Children as are fit objects to receive the advantages of this Institution.

THE Committee of Governors meet every *Saturday* Morning at Ten o'clock at the Foundling Hospital, to receive and deliberate on Petitions praying for the Admission of Children.

Children can only be received into this Hospital upon *personal* application of the Mothers.

Petitions must set forth the *true* State of the Mother's case; for if any deception is used the Petition will be rejected, and the Child will not be received into the Hospital.

No application can be received previous to the birth, nor after the Child is *Twelve months old.*

No Child can be admitted unless the Committee is satisfied, after due inquiry, of the *previous good character,* and present necessity of the Mother, and that the Father of the Child has *deserted* it and the Mother; and also, that the reception of the Child, will, in all probability, be the means of replacing the Mother in the course of virtue, and the way of an honest livelihood.

Persons who present Petitions to the Committee, must not apply to any Governor, or to any Officer or Servant belonging to the Hospital on the subject, on any pretence whatever; but they themselves must attend at NINE O'CLOCK on Saturday Morning at the Hospital with their Petitions; all of which will be considered in rotation, whilst the Petitoners are expected to remain in attendance.

No money is received for the admission of Children, nor any Fee or Perquisite allowed to be taken by any Officer of the Hospital, on pain of dismissal; and indeed any Person, who shall be known to offer the same, will subject her Petition to rejection; the Officers and Servants of the Hospital having been instructed to acquaint the Committee whenever such offer is made.

The Children of Married Women and Widows are not admissible into this Hospital.

The Petition on the other Half-Sheet of this Paper is to be filled up with Attention on the following Plan : the Blanks being numbered as a guidance. Blank marked (1) insert the name of the Petitioner. (2) Place of Residence. (3) Petitioner's Age. (4 and 5) Day and Month on which the Child was born. (6) Male or Female. (7) Father's Name. (8) His Trade or Occupation. (9) Place of Residence when first acquainted with the Petitioner. (10 and 11) When the Mother last saw him. (12) What is become of him.

NOTE.—Petitioners must not bring their Children with them until desired to do so.

How did Mary Anne Wingfield qualify to petition the London Foundling Hospital to admit her infant son? Petitions could not be made prior to the birth of the infant and not after his first birthday. She alone was responsible for her petition. She had to prove to the Inquirers and the Committee of Governors that the baby's father had deserted her and the baby. Every part of her petition had to be found to be true.

The Committee of Governors at the LFH was interested in assisting first-time, unwed mothers who lacked the means to provide for their child. Most importantly, the Committee had to have found in their inquiry that the petitioner had "previous good character." Only then would the LFH provide for and educate the child. The mother would therefore have a chance to be employed again and return to an appropriate and respectable life.

Jessica A. Sheetz-Nguyen's book, *Victorian Women, Unwed Mothers and the London Foundling Hospital*, provides a comprehensive study of the Foundling Hospital, including a description of the petition process. Sheetz-Nguyen notes that "The administrators of the Foundling Hospital reviewed over two hundred Petitions annually, deliberated on about one hundred cases, and accepted not more than twenty-five percent of all cases."

Mary Anne Wingfield had a preliminary review, followed by a formal hearing. Her application began August 8, 1870 and her infant was admitted three weeks later.

The following document is a copy of the actual petition made by Mary Anne Wingfield to the Committee of Governors of the London Foundling Hospital. Her baby boy was born May 6, 1870. She was 17 years old and unmarried. It states her home address. The baby's father was 22-year-old Charles Davis.

Birth of child is registered at Pimlico.

I.I.

To the Governors and Guardians of the
Hospital for the Maintenance and
Education of Exposed and Deserted
Young Children,

Staying with my parents. 8 months.

THE PETITION of (1) *Mary Anne Winfield*
of (2) *1 Nell Gwynne Cottages Grosvenor Row, Pimlico*
HUMBLY SHOWETH

That your Petitioner is unmarried, (3) *17* Years of
Age, and was on the (4) *6th* Day of (5) *May 1870*
delivered of a (6) *Male* Child, which is wholly
dependent on your Petitioner for its support, *being
deserted by the Father.*

Single. (22)

That (7) *Charles Davis* is the Father of
the said Child, and was, when your Petitioner became acquainted with him, a (8) *Footman* *Fellow Servant
at Capt. Wood R.N.*
(9) *21 Gloucester Street, Pimlico* and your Petitioner
last saw him on the (10) *13th* Day of (11) *May 1870*
and believes he is now (12) *gone to Australia*

Your Petitioner therefore humbly prays that you
will be pleased to receive the said Child into
the aforesaid Hospital.

Mary Anne Winfield

Mary Anne and Charles worked for the same household and its address is given. They were fellow servants. Charles Davis was employed as a footman, or male domestic worker. Mary Anne last saw him May 13, one week after the baby was born. After that, she believed Charles went to Australia. Her signature is at the bottom of the petition.

At the top of the petition, someone wrote, "Birth of child is registered at Pimlico." From the handwriting, it appears to have been written by James Twiddy, the Inquirer for Mary Anne Wingfield's case.

I did a search in findmypast.com. The section "England & Wales births 1837–2006 Transcription" shows Charles Davis, birth year 1870, birth quarter 2, London City. I believe Mary Anne named her baby after his father. She thought he would marry her and that they would raise the baby together.

In order to determine "previous good character," the Committee of Governors typically asked very personal questions during the hearing. Additionally, they were interested in statements from employers that spoke to the petitioner's record and work ethic. There were so few openings at the Foundling Hospital that they had to be sure the mother, when unburdened of her infant, would become employed again and lead a responsible life.

At some point, Mary Anne Wingfield made her statement in support of her petition to have her child admitted to the LFH. Her statement was recorded by a transcriber. I asked the LMA for help translating her statement. They were happy to help and asked me to scan and send the original copy back, because they did not have the funds to retrieve it again from the archives.

I sent my version along with the copy of the original. They could easily have spent more of my money, but instead they asked me to scan the statement for them. I love the LMA!

Here is the LMA's version of Mary Anne Wingfield's statement. "F" is the baby's father, Charles Davis.

> When first acquainted with the F, I was living with Captain Wood of 21 Gloucester Street in Pimlico as Homemaid. This was 2 years ago last Oct—The F came as footman serv. 1868—after 3 months he courted me and promised me marriage not known to the family. He seduced me in Oct 1869—in my room—When pregnant, I told him and he said he would make it all right. My mother discovered my pregnancy a fortnight before my child was born and spoke to the F. I left my workplace in Feb. My mistress now knows what has happened—The F left his place on his own accord. I was confined at my mother's, attended by Dr. Webb of 9 St. George's Road, Pimlico. If requested Mr. Wood will I think give a character letter.
>
> At Captain Wood's 16 months.

~

The Inquirer from the Committee of Governors, James Twiddy, wrote a statement in support of Mary Anne Wingfield's Petition. A few words are very difficult to read, but Mr. Twiddy included all the essential information for the Committee—information that supported the petitioner's plea to have her son admitted to the LFH.

He also asked for references from her employer, Captain Wood, her doctor, Ed. Webb, and the Rev. W. Rumsey. The opinions of each of these gentlemen were crucial for the success of Mary Anne's petition. Her case would be determined by Mr. Twiddy's statement and the three references, along with her petition and statement. All the details had to align for the Committee to ascertain the truth and make their decision.

Here is a copy of Mr. Twiddy's statement followed by the three references he requested:

13.8.70

Mary Anne Wingfield

Your Inquirer begs to report that he has seen petitioner's father and received from him a statement to the effect namely that petitioner is one of a family of eleven children, four of whom, including herself, are still upon his hands at home. That her mother, mainly supports the family as a washerwoman. That he has followed business of a coachman in private families all his life, but is now disabled by chronic rheumatism and can no longer continue his calling. The petitioner has always been well conducted and has maintained a good character in the service places where she has been in service. That there was nothing, apparently, against her character when she left the service of Captain Wood, and returned to her home on Feb 7 last, being out of health. That her condition of pregnancy was not discovered till up to the time of her confinement, when she made a statement regarding the paternity of her child, similar to that made by her to your Institution— That the father was immediately sought after with an order to bring him to terms regarding the future of petitioner. That the father visited petitioner a week after the birth of the child, and promised to marry her, but he never repeated his visit, and when requested after at Captain Wood's it was found that he had left his place suddenly, and nothing was known of him there as to his subsequent involvement— That he has now entirely deserted petitioner and her child, and there is no word of him left— That petitioner is quite unable to maintain herself and child, and that her parents are too poor to aid her effectively. That if relieved of her child by the F.H. she wants to be enabled to get another service at once, and it is confidently believed by her parents, would do well in future employment.

Your Inquirer has written for information upon this case to Captain Wood, Ed. Webb, and the Rev W. Rumsey respectively, and has received their answers to be found herewith—

James Twiddy

Reference from her employer, Captain Wood

21 Gloucester Street
Belgrave Road S.W.
August 14th (1870)

Captain Wood presents his Compliments to Mr. Twiddy and in reply to his letter left of late that Mary Anne Wingfield's statement is quite correct. While she was in his service, he considered her as honest and trustworthy and when she left, which she did about 3 months before the birth of her child he was quite unaware of what was likely obvious. Charles Davis left Captain Wood's toward the end of May and he is quite unable to state what has become of him. Captain Wood considers it would be a very charitable act of the Foundling Hospital to admit the child in question as its mother is one of a very large family and her parents are very poor, consequently she is obliged to work hard for her living.

—Captain Wood

Reference from the Rev W. Rumsey

Aug. 17. 1870

Dear Sir,

The story of Mary Anne Wingfield is unfortunately perfectly true. She and her family are well known to me. The parents and elder children have been always thoroughly respectable, and the fall of Mary Anne has been a very bitter grief to them.

The girl had an excellent character previously—and was a nice quiet servant. She lived in a fine family and the footman seduced her and when he found she was with child he suddenly left and disappeared.

M.A. Wingfield seems to be quite broken down by the consequence of her sin and most deserving of amendment. Therefore, if I might venture to say so, she seems to me a very fit case for the Committee of the F.H. to take into their favorable consideration.

I fear this will not add much to your information, but I trust it may be in some degree what you want.

Yours faithfully,

H.d. Rumsey

Reference from her doctor, Edw Webb

9 St. George's Road
Pimlico. S.W.
Aug. 18th, 1870 —

Dear Sir,

As far as I know from your letter the statements made by Mary Ann Wingfield of 1 Nell Gwynne Cottages are perfectly true — I have known the Family for nearly twenty years, I attended the young woman's mother in some of her confinements — I also attended a married sister in her first confinement. Her mother has worked for my Family as a laundress and I have therefore had numerous opportunities of judging of their general character — I believe them to be hardworking, honest, but very poor people and I never heard a word against the general character of the young woman — and in my opinion it is undoubtedly her first child —

I remain

Yours faithfully,
Edw Webb

Reportedly, my ancestors were very poor. They were raising eleven children. But they were hard working and well-respected in their community as well. Mary Anne was described as honest and trustworthy, a nice quiet servant with excellent character. I am proud to be part of the Wingfield clan.

~

The London Metropolitan Archives have the following statement at the end of every communication: "Please do not hesitate to contact us again if you have any further questions."

They helped me tremendously with the Transcriber Notes. They also answered the following questions I had about James's name.

Dear LMA,

I am very grateful for your helpful information. Thanks so much!

How did the Committee for the Foundling Hospital determine a new name for Mary Anne Wingfield's 3-month-old son? Was "James Thurnall" a name connected with the FH? This intrigues me, because a person's identity and heritage are inseparable and can be lost when children are renamed.

Thank you for your time and effort on my behalf.

Sincerely, Bonnie Parsons

London Metropolitan Archives reference: 2016/06139

Dear Ms. Parsons

Thank you for your recent email.

When children were baptised, usually on the first Sunday after their admission, names were chosen fairly randomly. The names given were sometimes that of a governor of the hospital or of a famous person. CG

Mary Anne Wingfield's Petition was accepted. The baby was admitted to the LFH. The separation had to have been heart-wrenching for the baby, his mother, and her family. But at the same time, Mary Anne believed her baby would have a better chance to survive. She and her family were unable to provide for him. Without the responsibility of parenting at age 17, she could get back to work to support herself and assist her family.

On August 29, 1870, Baby Charles Davis was baptized and named James Thurnall. I searched for a gentleman named Thurnall in the LFH history and found no one. It is a common name, so I did not pursue my search outside of the LFH.

The next mention of James is in the class list at the LFH when he was 10 years old. That list had led me to the London Foundling Hospital and all these discoveries!

～

October 29, 1884, at the age of 14, James began an apprenticeship with a hairdresser/barber, James Davies, in London. The LMA sent me a copy of the handwritten list with James's assignment. Interestingly, James's medical history and school reports were not saved. Being accepted into the LFH was the most important and impressive event. His mother's petition was flawless, and James's acceptance may have saved his life.

By the age of 30, James had moved to Swansea, Wales and was living in a boarding house. He soon met my great-grand-mother, Helen Louisa Gulliver, who was born and raised in Wales. They were married in April of 1903. Their only child, my grandmother, Frances Helen Thurnall, was born in 1906.

I know from Joan's sister, Doreen, that James Thurnall spent his entire career as a hairdresser/barber. My grandmother remembered him braiding her long red hair into "earphones." Doreen also recalled that James wrote letters to his daughter, saying that he wished they could come to Montreal to see her and her daughters, Joan and Doreen. Doreen said neither party had been able to afford the trip.

JOAN IN THE EARLY 1930'S

Helen Thurnall died in 1938 at the age of 72. James Thurnall died in 1947 at age 77. The Wales National Probate Calendar 1858–1966 states:

THURNALL James left an inheritance of the equivalent of $235.00 to Frances Helen Williamson.

I wish they had been able to visit one another. The years go by quickly, and then it is often too late. At least today, cellphones and internet chats help families stay in touch when visits are impossible for one reason or another.

~

During my search for James Thurnall, I wrote emails to family and friends about the LFH. It was an exciting and rewarding experience to receive Mary Anne Wingfield's Petition and learn about James's life. My friend, Liz Langland, is an author and scholar on the Victorian Era. Here is my email to her when I was finding out about James Thurnall.

Dear Liz,

I have a fascinating story for you about my great-grandfather, James Thurnall. He was born in London in 1870 to a desperately poor 17-year-old housemaid whose suitor, a 22-year-old footman for the same household, promised support and marriage then bolted to Australia after their son was born.

I paid London Metropolitan Archives to research James because I came across his name in a class list from the Foundling Hospital when he was 10 years old (ancestry.com). The LMA sent a lot of very interesting and very sad documents. Mary Anne Wingfield, the baby's mother, petitioned the Foundling Hospital to accept her baby. Among other documents, I received photocopies of her application and four letters from respectable community members supporting her application.

At 3 1/2 months, the baby was handed over by his mother, baptized, and named, James Thurnall. Further research led me to the original birth certificate. I believe my maternal great-great-grandmother named the baby after his father, Charles Davis. At that time, she was hoping he would marry her. I also believe she eventually married and had 5 more children, including a baby girl named Emily!

Here are excerpts from Liz's response.

Dear Bonnie,

What an amazing story!!! And how amazing that you were able to unearth it all.

And I am, indeed, quite familiar with the Foundling Hospital—certainly from all my study of the Victorian Age—but, wonderfully, during our last visit to London nine months ago, Jerry and I visited the Foundling Hospital, which now has a fantastic museum and exhibition. ... Every day, en route to the Tube at Russell Square, we passed the (former) Foundling Hospital—now a museum—and were, of course, lured into it. I found it sad that mothers had to petition for the hospital to take their infants. It must have torn them apart—but what were they to do?

One really must applaud the British for keeping such superb records. Imagine being able to locate your great-grandfather. You must, at some point, visit the Foundling Museum!

Yes, Liz. You're right!

19

MATERNAL HALF-SIBLINGS

My search for my birth family has evolved over the years. Initially, I needed to know about my birthmother. Even at an early age, when I pondered where I came from, I focused on my birthmother. After meeting Joan's family and becoming acquainted with them, I turned my attention to my birthfather.

Sadly, the adoption agency repeatedly refused to search for him. Even though Joan gave them his name, it did not appear on my birth certificate. I understand that it would have been very unusual at the time to put the father's name on the birth certificate of an illegitimate child.

Unbelievably, the agency did not want to search for him because he might not have known about me. I was told this by more than one adoption caseworker. Omissions, deceptions, and secrets! I kept reapplying until, after many years, they finally agreed to do a search in 2014. It was, however, too late. They claimed he died in 2010.

~

A year or so later, a search angel with Adoptees' Liberty Movement Association (ALMA) told me that my maternal half-siblings had a right to know that Joan had died from breast cancer. I believed they also had a right to know that her sister died from pancreatic cancer and her brother from lung cancer.

I knew Batshaw would not search for my half-siblings for the purpose of our knowing each other. However, I wanted to go ahead and get the medical information to them—pray for more, but expect less!

I had to start at the beginning again, with an application and forms and proofs of identity.

October 29, 2015

Adoption Program Manager:

Upon receipt, we will verify if we have files relating to your situation. If we do, your request will be added to our waiting list and you will be so informed. We will then notify you when we are ready to proceed with your request.

Sounds familiar! Here is my request to have Batshaw relay medical information to my half-siblings.

November 7, 2015

Dear Batshaw Adoption Caseworker,

Thank you for sending me the forms. I have completed two sets—one for my half-brother, born Robert Williamson, and a second for my half-sister, born Mary Frances Williamson.

My search for my birth families began in 1983. Both birthparents were deceased by the time I found them. My birthmother was only 54 and died from breast cancer in 1983. In 1988, I found her and visited her grave. My birth-father reportedly died at the age of eighty, five years ago.

My birthmother, Joan Helen Williamson, gave up four babies for adoption. I was born in Catherine Booth Hospital in 1949. Robert and Mary Frances were also born in Catherine Booth. A fourth baby was born around 1969 in Ormstown and Joan named her Shirley.

I want Robert and Mary Frances to know the medical history of their birthmother and her family. Also, I am sure you can understand what it would mean to me to meet them. My address and telephone numbers are on file for them to contact me. And please feel free to give them my email.

Finally, please accept my heartfelt gratitude for every-thing you and Ville Marie/Batshaw have done over the thirty-two plus years I have been searching and that you continue to do for me. My search has been for my natural identity and heritage and now, my siblings.

Thanks again for all your help.

Sincerely yours,
Bonnie Parsons

My packet to Batshaw included information from Joan's doctors and her death certificate.

In January 2016, I received written confirmation that they had received everything from me. "You will be contacted by one of our adoption caseworkers in the near future, who will explain to you the process pertaining to your situation."

By May, I still had not heard from Batshaw, and so I called and left a voicemail. A worker returned my call on May 20th. Here are my notes from that day:

Takeaways:

- Staff doctors have given the approval for Batshaw to search for Robert and Mary Frances to give them medical information on Joan and maybe other family histories.
- She said she was making this a *priority*.
- If my sibs want to communicate with me, I will be asked to write the first letter of what they call "Letter Exchange." My letters will go through the Batshaw police!
- Clearly, they do not like matching up siblings.
- Tons of protocol and many managers.
- I won't hear until their searches are done for both half-siblings.
- After the call—I felt such sudden anger.
- I felt like my requests to inform my half-siblings of medical histories and connect with them was criminal.
- I heard little understanding and no respect.

I was extremely stunned by her manner and all the rules—my anger just jumped out of me after I hung up.

In September, I called for an update! After four months, I was questioning the *priority* status of my case. Batshaw refuses emails and phone calls! But I have to say, if you want to reach someone, leave a voicemail!

The next day, I received a call and she reported that she had relayed the information! Just like that—done! She refused to confirm that she spoke to both of my half-siblings, but after a couple of slips of plural pronouns, I believed she reached them.

She claimed she sent them "official letters fairly recently," written verifications of the information she gave them over the phone. I gathered there were conversations. One of them was not surprised to hear that his or her birthmother had relinquished more than one child. *What's that all about?*

Sadly, I feel that she may have had an intimidating tone during her phone call. However, I was relieved to know my half-siblings were alive.

It was so frustrating that this stranger talked to them when I was not permitted to even know their names. I'm not sure if they know they can contact Batshaw to begin a conversation with me. I am sure the worker offered no encouragement or further information about me or how I would love to exchange letters.

I knew I had to write back. I wanted to chronical my personal journey—a journey that is very familiar to you by now, but also invaluable in making an impression on someone who had the potential to make a real difference in my search.

September 28, 2016

Dear Batshaw,

Thank you for returning my call today. Through your work, I trust that you have a clear understanding of the issues surrounding identity loss for adoptees. The importance of a human being's heritage cannot be denied. One's DNA cannot be erased and replaced like scribbles on a chalkboard. Identity is, therefore, hugely important for many adult adoptees who have an innate need to know their heritage.

My search for my birthparents began in 1983. Five years later, I received a call from Ville Marie that my birthmother died in 1983, three months after my request for a search! We could have met.

Now I was determined to find her name and the family. With a couple of identity clues from Ville Marie, pre-internet, I drove from Buffalo, New York to the Toronto Reference Library. I found her full name in her obituary—Joan Helen Williamson.

As you can imagine, I treasure Joan's and my similarities, and I am forever grateful to Joan's family for welcoming me and my family.

In 2014, after three decades and four search applications, I finally received a call from Batshaw reporting that my birthfather was deceased only four years earlier! Another missed opportunity. In my home, with the internet and again a couple of clues from Ville Marie/Batshaw over the years, I was able to find his name in his obituary—Ronald Kelly.

A kind-hearted family friend has told me about him and I have one photo from the funeral home. Now I know that both of my birthparents are deceased and that their privacy protection is no longer necessary.

Joan Helen Williamson relinquished three more babies after I was born. It is wonderful that you were able to contact the male born in 1953--Joan named him Robert, and the female born in 1955--Joan named her Mary Frances. The last baby, a female, Shirley, was born in Ormstown around 1969. I have no idea if you were able to contact her with the medical histories.

Robert, Mary Frances, and I are all in our sixties. Joan and all three birthfathers are deceased. Their privacy protection is again no longer necessary.

Are there laws of privacy protection that extend beyond the birthparents? Please send me a copy of your privacy protection laws regarding birthparents and others.

In the event that there aren't any privacy protection laws that still apply, now that the birthparents are deceased, I formally request my original adoption file, including all identifying information. My adoptive parents, Don and Mary Fairbairn, are also deceased.

I request the names and telephone numbers of the two half-siblings with whom you spoke. Please keep in mind that I am now an adult. These privacy decisions were made when I was an infant, sixty-seven years ago! Obviously, I do not need your protection any longer. My half-siblings are also adults now.

It is unnecessary for letters to be passed through your office and checked for inappropriate information. I was an educator for thirty-eight years. My husband and I raised two children, now successful adults. They are aghast that you want to check my letters for appropriateness. As I say, please remember, I am an adult adoptee, not an infant.

I look forward to hearing from you and/or your manager.

Sincerely,
Bonnie Parsons

Frustration!

"I fought the law, and the law won!"
—Sonny Curtis of the Crickets, 1960.

It became clear to me that my logical argument regarding privacy laws did not apply to adoption searches in the Province of Quebec.

I did receive a response from Batshaw. It contained internet links to Quebec laws regarding privacy. As they say in the world of the internet, the links were *not user friendly!* I thought of asking for more precise links, pages numbers, or photocopies of the laws. But in truth, I was out of steam.

20

PATERNAL HALF-SIBLINGS?

I have often said in this memoir that I successfully identified my birthfather in 2014. After all, the agency gave me enough information to search the Montreal obituaries. The social worker was clearly taken aback when I gave her Ronald Kelly's name. She promised to tell me if the common Irish name I found was off base—Kelly was apparently not off base!

Cousin Lillian confirmed that the gentleman in my photo was him. Facebook's *DNA Detectives* members said they saw resemblances in the photos of Ronald and me. What more am I looking for? *I wanted further proof—DNA proof!* I knew, however, that the odds were against me finding a potential biological relative to agree to DNA testing.

Lillian's and my DNA mismatch had been a major disappointment. I promised her I would not be upset if the results weren't what we wanted, but still, it was a setback. I wondered if I would ever know why Lillian and I do not share DNA. I spent hours searching for the answer, and I learned many intriguing facts and details, but not enough to determine why we do not match. I decided to resume a focus on Ronald Kelly and me!

The Montreal family friend was the one who first suggested the answer could be found in DNA. Both she and Lillian were strongly opposed to me contacting Ronald's children. I cooperated at first, but then I needed to move forward.

It was a very slow and painstaking process. I reached out with Facebook "friend" requests and messages. I waited and deleted and tried again and waited again.

The oldest and closest sibling in age to me did not respond to my message. In all fairness, I don't think he spends much time on Facebook. My next move was to reach out to his daughter, because I could tell she used Facebook regularly.

"Hi Annie, I am working on my family heritage. I left a message for your father on his Facebook page, but I am not sure he has found it. Could you please ask him to look for it?

Thanks very much,
Bonnie Parsons"

Seven months later, she wrote to me! My first real breakthrough. Here is our conversation (I've made minor changes because her first language is French, not English):

"Hi Bonnie, My father is not sure of your story. This is a shock for him. Contact Joanne. She is the sister of my father. Sorry I am not good in English. Annie"

I responded, elated!

"Hi Annie, Thank you for writing back to me. That is so sweet of you. Good job on the English!! I understood everything! I will write to Joanne tomorrow. Thanks again, Bonnie"

She had signed off with a smiling monkey sticker. I left her a happy Snoopy. I was ecstatic with her message. The smiling monkey put me over the top! Snoopy is a Parsons family favorite, and I knew she'd love it.

The next day I wrote: "Hi Annie—Here is what I sent to Joanne. I want you to have a copy, too!" My letter included my photo of Ronald Kelly from the funeral home next to one of myself.

Hi Joanne,

I appreciate Annie's suggestion that I contact you. I hope you are ok with it! I was adopted in Montreal by a wonderful family. But like most adoptees, I have a natural interest in my heritage. I learned my birth mother's identity in 1988. She died from cancer in 1983. Two years ago the adoption agency told me my birth father, who had a common Irish name, died in late 2010 in Montreal at the age of 80. I searched the paper and Ronald Kelly was the only gentleman who died at 80, at that time.

My birth parents were teenagers when I was born. They met at a dance in the summer of 1948. I was born in April 1949.

Annie's response to the photos: "Wow! I am in shock. Your real father is my grandpa Ronald. I'll ask my mom for more pictures of Ronald. Annie"

These developments were stunning and thrilling! I wrote back: "Hi Annie, I would love to see more pictures of Ronald! Thanks so much, Bonnie"

Kindness was coming my way! What a different feeling.

～

Even though I didn't hear from Annie or Joanne for a while, my contact with Annie gave me such encouragement. It really changed everything. It was a new beginning for me.

I reached out to Annie again two months later. Marc translated my letter into French. Here's the English version.

Hi Annie,

I wish you and your family a Happy New Year. My cousin, Marc, has kindly agreed to translate this message from me to you. I know that adoption is a difficult topic for families.

I grew up in a wonderful family. They loved me as if they had given me life. They understood that I have a right to know my heritage, my biological background, and medical history. Most importantly, they never questioned my appreciation for the upbringing they gave me.

After I had my son and daughter, I asked my mom and dad where I should begin the search for information about my birthparents. They sent me the Montreal agency address immediately. At the time, I was strangely feeling a connection with my birthmother. Later I learned that she was on her deathbed and died from breast cancer less than three months after I began my search.

She died in 1983. I also asked for information about my birthfather. Over thirty years and many requests later, I was told that he died in 2010. I never met either of my birthparents. I welcome DNA testing to confirm that Ronald Kelly is my birthfather.

Thank you for being sweet and kind. My cousin has agreed to translate a message back to me.

Sincerely,
Bonnie

I believe Annie handed over the reins to Joanne when she asked me to write to her. Joanne is possibly a half-sister, and so I completely understood Annie's decision.

~

Four months after I sent my letter and photos to Joanne— with a copy to Annie—Joanne wrote back! I'll never forget the moment I saw her message. I was so thrilled with excitement, appreciation, and even disbelief. I will always remember the moment; I simply don't have the words to express it.

Joanne: Hi Bonnie, I am so sorry I haven't answered before. I guess I was shocked, but I have been thinking of your message every day since I received it. I would gladly do a DNA test to get the answer you are looking for.

Bonnie: I am so happy to hear from you! Thank you for getting back to me. Yes, DNA would answer the question. AncestryDNA is the best company, but there are 2 other big companies: Family Tree DNA and 23andMe.

Do you think your father and I look alike?

We had long messaging chats every night over the next week. We shared information and photos of our families. She learned that we named our son Ron.

I explained my searches. Here are further highlights.

Joanne: I am sorry you found out about your birthparents after they passed away. My father was a great man. I was always his little princess. I was the baby. I am now close to 46 years old and I have two great kids: a daughter who will turn 17 in May and my son who's 14.

Bonnie: I am so happy to learn about your kids.

Joanne: I would love to do the DNA test. I am at my mom's now, but I will get back to you for sure.

Bonnie: Thanks, Joanne. And thanks again for getting back to me. That was so kind of you!

Joanne: (later that evening) And yes, I do see the resemblance between you and my father.

I was, once again, overwhelmed. I felt I was getting closer to knowing—knowing for sure. I apologized for not being able to message her in French.

Joanne: No worries about the French. I speak and read English. I may not have the right grammar though.

I researched ways to purchase a DNA kit for Joanne. AncestryDNA isn't able to accept US dollars for a kit going to Canada. In the end, we thought it best for Joanne to order her own kit, and I would mail her a check the next day.

Joanne: I ordered my DNA test.

Bonnie: Great. I think this is the way to go. You will have all your results. It's fun to see where your ancestors came from.

Joanne: I can't wait to find out now.

Joanne: Btw—This is my gift to you. I'm sorry I haven't answered you before.

Bonnie: Dear Joanne, please reconsider—I would be really happy to pay for your kit.

Joanne: That's very nice of you. I feel I owe this to you. I owe you the answer you are looking for for so long.

Bonnie: I am overwhelmed by your kindness and thoughtfulness.

Joanne: It's my pleasure really.

Bonnie: I can't wait to know the results.

Joanne: Same here. I'm sure you had great parents, but I can understand wanting to know who your biological family is.

Bonnie: Exactly. Thanks for understanding.

Joanne: I will do my best to answer your questions.

Bonnie: Thanks, I am so sorry your father left you when he did.

Joanne: Thanks. My father had a good life. He had the chance to meet his grandchildren and great-grandchildren.

For St. Patrick's Day, I sent Joanne an e-card. It included many of the symbols of Ireland to the tune of "Danny Boy." I wanted to thank her for getting back to me as well as to honor her Irish heritage.

Joanne: A lot of memories are coming back since this weekend and I started missing my dad so much. I always tried to be strong for everybody and I never really cried after my father's death until last night.

Bonnie: When my mom died, I spoke at the service and said she is still with us but with a new address. And I spoke to her.

Joanne: When my father passed away, he didn't want a service at church and I always joked, saying I will make a big Irish party for his funeral. My last words at the party were, "Let's raise our glass to my father's new life," while the song "Oh Danny Boy" was playing.

Bonnie: I am so impressed. You are a great daughter.

Joanne: Thank you.

~

Our conversation turned to the spirit world when I told her about Joan's presence at my reading in Lily Dale, New York.

Bonnie: After my parents died, Paul and I went to Lily Dale, a community of mediums, south of Buffalo. I got a reading from a medium. She said she wouldn't comment on my adoptee situation which was fine with me. Then after a while, she said my birthmother refused to leave and wanted me to know she was so sorry she couldn't keep me. The medium explained to me that the stronger the love that was shared, the stronger the communication you feel at a reading. My mom and I were always close, and she never left during the entire session! Now I'm told that Joan was there, too.

Joanne: My mom believes a lot in spirits and mediums.

Bonnie: Your mom and I would get along.

Joanne: Very much.

Bonnie: I chatted with Emily today. She was able to work from home because of the snowstorm. She is very excited that you got back to me. She said you are so pretty!! Of course! We are very close. Like you, Emily does not judge.

Joanne: She looks like a very nice person. She is very pretty too, and I'm impressed with the 12 marathons.

I used to go to bootcamp.

I need to start working out again.

Who are we to judge?!

Bonnie: Whatever happens for you and me, I know your dad is with you. He is blessed to have a devoted daughter like you.

Joanne: Thank you. It means a lot to me. He would have been so proud to know that his first grandson was named Ronald.

Bonnie: Joanne! Now you've got me!

Joanne: When I was born, my mom wanted to name me Martine and my father said, would you mind if we call her Joanne.

Bonnie: Wow!

Joanne: My mom told me this weekend that he had mentioned to her that his first love was when he was 18 years old. They couldn't get married because she had to move. I have a funny feeling my father never knew Joan was pregnant and her parents sent her away.

Bonnie: OMG

Joanne: I know. She didn't have the name of the girl, just that story. But it makes sense, doesn't it?

Bonnie: Please tell your mom, "thanks."

Joanne: I will.

Bonnie: Sometimes I think that the chances of him knowing she was pregnant were slim. I always wonder. They were strictly religious, and Joan was kept inside and then sent away.

Joanne: I wish he was here to answer all your questions. Religion was ruling everything and everybody at that time.

Bonnie: You are so sweet, and I know he was too. xo

Joanne: Good night xx

~

Bonnie: (next day) Dear Joanne, It has been an amazing and emotional 4 days. There is something about you—your thoughtfulness and kindness are amazing and I am very grateful. Emily said this afternoon that she is so excited for me after all these years and hard work that you got back to me and you are who you are! I believe there is a gene for kindness and non-judgmentalism, and that quality makes people around you feel accepted and happy. Please don't feel you have to respond—I just want to let you know that my family and I are so grateful.

Joanne: Thank you. You are right, it has been 4 emotional days. I relived memories from childhood and I thank you for that. I just can't wait for the DNA test, but at the same time, I feel that I don't need it. I felt a connection with you right away.

Bonnie: Yes, I feel the same way. With Joan, my search was right without DNA testing. Now I feel my search was right again. Hopefully DNA will confirm it. An adoption search angel found an ancestry.com site by Lillian. Her tree had your dad and Wesley and another brother.

Joanne: Robert. He passed away in '69 I think. He had a kidney transplant and passed away a year after. He was a professional golf player.

Bonnie: Lillian knew about that. Yes, a great athlete. She told me about Bobby's kidney transplants.

Joanne: Wow. That was with ancestry.com?

Bonnie: Yes. Lillian knew we named our son Ron. I shared that with her. There's one more thing Lillian said.

Joanne: What is it?

Bonnie: Lillian said, "I believe Ron is your father because of two signs from God—you named your son Ron and he is now a kidney transplant surgeon."

Joanne: Omg, my father was supposed to give his kidney, but it was more complicated. I don't know why, so Wesley did. It's crazy all the signs and similarities.

Bonnie: I didn't know when the right moment would come along to tell you about Lillian. I hope you are ok. It is a lot to absorb.

Joanne: No worries. I'm glad to know.

Bonnie: Maybe Lillian has a point or two. It is all too surreal. We wish we knew for sure now, maybe we do. We'll see.

Joanne: I think we do. We'll have a confirmation in a few weeks.

Joanne: next day: Happy Saint Patrick's Day!

Bonnie: Thanks, Joanne! I'm wearing my favorite green sweater! Have a great weekend. Ron was so happy to hear the update last night. Charlie's birthday is Monday, so it is a birthday weekend.

Joanne: Happy Birthday Charlie

Bonnie: Say, "hi" to your mom.

Joanne: I will. She is very happy that I finally answered you.

Bonnie: Me too!

Joanne: And me too. I am sorry I haven't done it before.

Bonnie: I really understand. Please don't worry about it. It just means so much to me that we are now communicating. I am also very thankful to your mom for supporting me.

~

Our conversations continued. We learned family birthdays. Joanne and her mom have April birthdays--Joan's and my birthdays are in April, too. This led to further astonishing revelations.

Bonnie: Joan gave birth to me on April 7th and turned 20 on the 22nd. So, she wasn't really a child.

Joanne: So, she was older then my father. My father was born in 1930.

Bonnie: Yes, she was about a year older, I think. They really weren't kids. I mean, maybe it really was love.

Joanne: I don't think so, I know so--with the story my mom told me last weekend.

Bonnie: Omg—my speculation was so off because I knew nothing.

Joanne: I learned about that story only this weekend.

Bonnie: My entire thinking is different now because of what your mom said. I always assumed they had a fling and that was it—one night.

Joanne: No, apparently there's a picture somewhere of them together at a wedding. Not sure who has that picture now, I think it's my sister. I will do my best to try to find pictures. Unfortunately, that's all I know. My father never talked too much about his past.

Bonnie: Joan was very private, too. The biggest clue the agency slipped to me back in 1988 was from my birth grandmother when they contacted her, she said, "Joan always kept to herself." With that clue, we found her last name in the obituaries up in Toronto.

Joanne: And what was her last name?

Bonnie: Williamson

Joanne: I don't know how you found out with that clue. omg

Bonnie: I knew from the agency that she died in 1983, her dad died before her, she had 2 sisters and a brother.

Joanne: So young to die.

Bonnie: I became obsessed about her—this is where your mom would understand ... I had inquired in May 1983. So, in the summer of 1983, I could not get her out of my mind,

Joanne: And that's when she passes away.

Bonnie: Yes. Then in 1988, they told me she died in 1983! I could have visited her at the end of her life. She died of breast cancer. We could have had 2 months together. That's what frustrates me about the adoption laws.

Joanne: 4 years in a row I did the 60 km walk to raise money for breast cancer.

Bonnie: Thank you, Joanne. My mom died from it too. She was so bright right until she needed Hospice care.

～

Bonnie: Joan was required to care for me for 6 weeks and then I went into foster care. She visited me in foster care and asked for photos. After 6 months, she was required to make a decision. I was adopted at 8 months. I believe we bonded in those 6 weeks. Then, years later, she wouldn't leave my session with the medium because she wanted me to know she didn't want to give me up.

Joanne: When did you find out you were adopted?

Bonnie: My parents always told me I was adopted.

Joanne: And I believe that when she died, she was with you and that's why you were thinking so much about her in 1983.

Bonnie: Joanne, you are so kind and sweet.

Joanne: Thank you.

Bonnie: I felt she was with me.

Joanne: And I believe it. A few years ago, one of my friends wanted to go see a card reader and she could speak to spirits. Of course, I was skeptical, but I still went with my friend. I was taking notes for her and she for me. When I asked about my father, she said your father is proud of you. But what shocked me is that she was talking to us in French all the time and when I asked about him, she start talking in English. She said that my father said, in rough times, just wear your necklace, it will give you strength. My father gave me that necklace that belonged to my grandma. It is a medallion that you can open. In it is my grandfather's picture and Uncle Bob. I started believing after that.

Bonnie: Wow. The medium knew about the medallion?

Joanne: We called the night before for an appointment and we only gave our first names. She knew nothing about us.

Bonnie: Amazing!

Joanne: My mom believes in angels also. She gave me a card to put in my wallet with the angel related to my birthday. Xo

Joanne and I continued our messaging. We were waiting for her to receive the AncestryDNA kit. It finally arrived at the end of March 2017. We were both surprised that her sample went off to Ireland for analysis—a pleasant irony. The Ancestry Corporate Headquarters are in Lehi, Utah. But then I discovered that the International Headquarters are in Dublin,

Ireland. It would be six to eight weeks before she received her results.

~

Bonnie: I am so excited that we share April birthdays

Joanne: My mom is also in April

Bonnie: I remember. Isn't it amazing? Joan was April 22nd, too. I saw an ad on Facebook for a t-shirt "Queens are born in April"

Joanne: Love it! I need a t-shirt like that

And then we exchanged birthday wishes—first of many, I hoped.

Joanne: Happy Birthday Bonnie I wish you all the best. Enjoy your weekend with Emily

Bonnie: Happy Birthday, Joanne! Have a great day.

~

My newfound first cousin, Marc, and I keep up through emails and delightful phone chats. I feel so blessed. We've felt like cousins from the first time we talked. He signed off recently, "Well my dear cousin, enjoy your day." Thank you, DNA!

As fellow adoptees, we share the same emotions and thoughts and the drive to discover our heritage. We understand that families have secrets. We may be the secret! But that shouldn't mean we cannot know our roots.

We still have the right to our identities and original birth certificates. We want to know the circumstances of our births. After years of searching, we know who our birthmothers are. Marc's and my DNA match appears to be on our birthfathers' side. Hopefully Joanne's DNA results will help both of us.

In the meantime, Marc was a joy to know—a funny, clever, no nonsense guy. I love his happy uplifting spirit.

~

Joanne and I continued to chat on Facebook messaging. We grew closer and more hopeful with each day. It took *forever* for her AncestryDNA kit to arrive. Then it took *forever* again for her results to arrive. We both wanted desperately for the DNA to prove that Ronald Kelly was my birthfather, that Joanne and I were sisters (albeit half-sisters), and that Joan and Ronald had been in love.

Finally, in mid-June, Joanne wrote, "***Hi Bonnie. My results are in***. So, we have an extremely high match. You are the first one on top of the list. But they say 2nd cousin. Could it be because we would be half-sisters?"

"YES!! Omg, omg, omg," I said, at which point we were both crying.

I was trying to maintain a little composure—Paul and I were on the Cross Sound Ferry, heading from Long Island, NY to Connecticut and then up to his mother's home in Massachusetts. We were in a booth, surrounded by fellow travelers. I can never get an internet signal on the ferry. This time I was more frustrated than ever! Joanne is new to Ancestry. I desperately wanted to see the results for myself! I was dying to log on. She would appear right between Emily and Marc! I couldn't wait.

I explained to Joanne that we were on the ferry and I couldn't see the results on my phone.

She replied, "I understand. It's a big weekend for you. We will have time to catch up. Maybe you could come to Montreal soon."

I was a little anxious now and tried to get more information from Joanne. "What is the cM? Click on me, then on the "i" in the gray circle."

"I don't see it," she said.

"Under 'predicted relationship,' click on my name first," I said.

That evening, Joanne wrote, "I just had a glass of champagne to my new sister (heart)."

And the next morning, I replied, "Awwww thanks, I wish I could have joined you ... I still can't see your results ... Were you able to register and activate?" I was like a kid Christmas morning waiting to see the tree.

"Working on it now," she said.

I had my laptop and Paul and I were in the hotel with internet! Joanne and I tried everything and found nothing. Eventually I called AncestryDNA and they said it could take a few days for the updates of new matches to appear. They said Joanne had done everything correctly.

So, I moved on as best I could and asked about her mom.

"She is excited. She's very emotional and she can't wait to meet you."

"Maybe she will see a resemblance in me to your dad," I said.

"We already do with your picture," said Joanne.

So exciting!! Joanne called her brother. Interestingly, he is an avid fisherman. Paul, my dad, and brother all loved fishing, so this is exciting news. I asked Joanne if he was surprised to hear about the DNA results.

"He was surprised I did the test. He's happy to know he has a new sister. It's very emotional for me, because I lost track of my brothers and sister when my father passed away. You are reuniting us. Thank you."

Joanne and her brother got together for dinner. They had a wonderful time discussing all the details and coincidences—naming our son Ron and Bobby's kidney transplants. Even though Joanne, her mom, and brother were thrilled in their own right, Joanne never forgot that this was my search and I was finally finding my birthfather. She was so happy for me!

~

Our conversations continued, and we shared information about our kids and their interests and activities. At the end of the week, I wrote to Joanne. It was Saturday morning, June 24, 2017:

Hi Joanne, One week ago, while we were on the Cross Sound Ferry, you got your DNA results!! I thought I would see them immediately, but I am still waiting. Would you mind clicking 3 times on your results for me? First click on your "View all your DNA matches." Here is mine with the top 4 (screenshot). Then click on my name. I'll click on Emily (screenshot). Last, click on the gray circle with the "I" (screenshot). I'd like to know your top 4 and then what is attached to the "i." All of this will be available to me when you show in my matches, but I'm so anxious waiting this long (smile). Thanks a million!!!

Joanne could not find the lowercase "i." There was also a misunderstanding about AncestryDNA results and Ancestry Family Trees. We shared logins for everything, but it took a while before we were focused solely on DNA results. Joanne was doing all this for me. I knew how confusing it could be. I had years of practice and determination as I searched for my birthfather. Joanne was trying, out of the kindness of her heart, to comprehend everything so that she *clicked* where I asked her to *click!* She had an appointment to keep and promised to work on it later.

~

Saturday afternoon, Joanne sent me an AncestryDNA invitation to view her DNA results. This way, she didn't have to worry about where to click—I could view everything on my own.

Bonnie: ***I am not there!***

Joanne: What? You are my highest match.

In fact, Ronald's cousin, Lillian, was Joanne's highest match. Lillian and I didn't match, and now Joanne and I do not match. Only Lillian and Joanne match! Joanne saw my log-in ID and New York State address under Lillian's name, a name she was not familiar with. I was the administrator of Lillian's test when she wasn't feeling well. Joanne was so excited, she didn't realize Lillian was her match, not me.

Joanne: OMG. When I saw your ID in Long Island, I was so sure. Are you ok? I am so sorry.

Bonnie: I will be ok.

Joanne: I am so sorry. I feel awful.

Bonnie: Don't feel awful. You're new to this. I will always be so grateful that you got tested.

We were both devastated. But we were also confused. We thought I looked like her dad, our daughters looked like sisters, we named our son Ron! But for me, the biggest confusion revolved around the obituary the agency led me to and their letter to me describing Ronald Kelly's death. His illnesses, the date he died, the funeral all belonged to Ronald Kelly.

Joanne wanted the two of us to have blood tests done. She was starting to doubt the validity of the saliva tests done in Ireland! I told her I would look into it.

My first major task that afternoon was to retrace my steps. I researched again the common Irish surnames and cross checked them in the *Montreal Gazette* with all obituaries in November and December 2010.

As Joanne said, "All the dots are connecting. There has to be an explanation."

We agreed that Joan did not knowingly lie to the agency. Saturday, June 24th came to a close and we both decided to try and get some sleep.

Sunday morning, we were back at it—trying to figure out why we did not match, even though everything pointed to her dad, Ronald Kelly, was my birthfather. Lillian had been sure he was. The adoption caseworker at the agency told me that super coincidences, or synchronicity, is common in adoption cases. She was not surprised that we named our son Ron.

Here's what I wrote to Joanne that morning:

Bonnie: I believe Joan thought Ronald was the father and that is why the agency information matches the obituary. I believe they dated for a while ... We have no way of knowing at this time how she became pregnant or with whom—it may or may not have been consensual. We can still believe in the relationship Joan and Ronald had.

Joanne: I was thinking exactly the same thing.

She also reminded me that her dad had insisted on naming her Joanne, which she thinks was in memory of Joan.

Then I wrote, "Once I realized that Joan told what she thought was the truth, I feel better. She was dating

Ronald and found out she was pregnant. At some point, she was sent to a home for unwed mothers. She is my birthmother, but unfortunately Ronald appears not to be my birthfather."

Joanne and members of my family still wanted us to have blood tests done. I never felt compelled to go that route. Joanne and Lillian matched. Lillian and Ronald were first cousins. Therefore, Joanne had to match Lillian. That was undeniably correct.

Joanne: You will always be my sister from NY.

Bonnie: DNA isn't the whole story.

Joanne: Exactly.

21

MORE DNA MATCHES

Joanne and I had difficulty letting go. We were holding onto a phantom DNA match that would have proven her dad was my birthdad, and she and I were half-sisters. After all, we felt like sisters! Over time, we had shared family news and photos.

We look forward to meeting some day for coffee or a glass of wine to celebrate our *sisterhood*.

I am left with this thought: How unfortunate that Batshaw thought Ronald Kelly was my birthfather. Their error led to so many misunderstandings: Ellen at Batshaw didn't deny the surname Kelly, Vicki discovered Lillian's family tree on ancestry.com, a dear friend gave a wonderful description of Ronald's character, many people observed that Ronald and I looked related, and Joanne's mother remembered the story of Ronald's first love when he was 18. Joanne's AncestryDNA results were at first confusing. And then our shared high hopes were shattered. If the friend had gotten DNA results from a Kelly, as she suggested I needed, the Batshaw error would have been caught over two years earlier!

I am *forever* grateful to Joanne for buying her own DNA kit and hanging in there for me. Her kindness far exceeded my dreams. Our friendship is precious to both of us and always will be.

~

Three weeks later, I received a new match in AncestryDNA. It fell between my daughter and Marc in my match list—exactly where I had expected to see Joanne's name, but this match is on my maternal side. It was a female—a strong match, high enough to be a half-sister. I realized that it had to be another one of Joan's relinquished babies!

I was elated and immediately wrote to her. Sadly, she did not respond. I sent a couple of emails throughout the summer. I was disappointed, but I know how important it is to be patient. Adoptees need time to absorb new information, and it is nothing short of very scary to make contact with someone who may be a blood relative after you have lived your life for over sixty years not knowing your birth family. And your only blood relatives are your own children, if you are a parent.

As time went on, however, I wondered why someone would send their saliva to AncestryDNA if they did not want to know the results.

In October, it became clear when I received an email from one of her daughters. I have changed their names to protect their privacy.

Caitlin introduced herself as the daughter of my high match and explained that she and her sister, Margo, were anxious to know their mother's genetic background. Their mother was born in Montreal and adopted in 1955. The sisters convinced their mother to get her DNA tested at AncestryDNA. The last thing they expected was a close DNA match!

I was so excited to respond. "When I saw your mother's DNA right under my daughter's, I was thrilled. The DNA matches for half-sisters. I believe your mom is the baby born in 1955 to Joan Helen Williamson from Verdun." Joan named her Mary Frances. I will call her Mary in this memoir.

Margo later sent me a text in Facebook messaging. She confirmed that she and her sister were only interested in their mother's ethnic heritage. They were surprised to see the high genetic match between Mary and me. In fact, they were not expecting any matches. The AncestryDNA results sparked something in the sisters. They now shared a curiosity I knew only too well!

~

AncestryDNA results include an Ethnicity Estimate they call your DNA Story. It shows a map of the globe and where your ancestors lived. It also has historical information. For example, it explains how people migrated to different regions. It describes what life was like during each time period. As an adoptee, it had never occurred to me that someone would have their DNA tested for the Ethnicity Estimate alone. For me, the purpose was to identify blood relatives, and better yet, close relatives. The higher the number of shared chromosomes the better!

Now I have a clearer understanding of how Mary's daughters persuaded her to get her DNA tested. When the results arrived, imagine their amazement when they saw our high match.

Unfortunately, Mary never wished to receive this information. She accepted the meaning of her closed adoption, and she was terribly afraid of hurting her family. Margo believes that her mother may be curious. However, Mary will not respond to me. The loyalty she has for her adoptive mother is greater than her curiosity about her birthmother and siblings. At least that's it for now.

I told Margo that I am available to discuss this with Mary. I still have great respect for my parents' feelings and they died in 2000 and 2001.

Things are so different now with the internet and DNA testing. Many people are finding that it is not wrong to check out your heritage from a closed adoption.

Margo and I have kept in touch. I shared family medical history and photographs. They know how lucky they are to have their mother's and my match. And yes, they share my curiosity. In particular, Margo asked about Joan relinquishing four babies. This is a sensitive topic for me, as I covered in Chapter 15. It gets to the core of the tragedies Joan endured. I am very protective of Joan's legacy. I will explain the circumstances in her life whenever I'm asked, so that she gets the respect I feel she deserves.

As I learned more about birthmothers and the suffering they endure, I felt empathy for Joan, and I had greater compassion for her decisions. I realized that, without support around her, adoption was her only option.

I explained to Margo that Joan's relinquishing four babies was the toughest thing for me to grasp. It had taken me a very long time. Over the years, I have written pieces of my memoir and struggled to articulate why Joan made her traumatic choices.

I took a reading break from writing a couple of years ago. My enlightenment came as I *listened* to birthmothers—their grief and sorrow doesn't just go away, often for a lifetime. The more I read, the more compassion I felt. Joan was uneducated as we know it today. At best, she finished 7th grade and then had business training. She was the oldest child in a strict religious family. They were very respected in the community and I know her pregnancy with me caused them great shame. I am also sure she wanted to keep me, but her parents would not allow it and insisted on an "adoption plan." She visited me in foster care and asked for photos. Given that she had little education, it is a miracle she was not pregnant again until four years later. Without birth control, she found herself pregnant three times following my birth. And for reasons we have no way of knowing, she did not marry.

The bottom line for me is that I believe she did the best she could in difficult and heartbreaking circumstances. She suffered greatly and later endured years of surgery and treatments for breast cancer leading to her early death at the age of 54.

It was the late 1940s and Joan's parents felt ashamed when she became pregnant. Pregnancy out of wedlock was completely unacceptable at that time in Quebec. There was no such thing as community support for an unwed mother and her infant. Joan had little education and no birth control—a bad combination, but she was a good person. Her family was very important to her and she was generous and kind.

I think she grew to accept that adoption was her only option--thus, the suffering.

Joan had a common-law marriage for at least the last fifteen years of her life. He is deceased now, but I had one conversation with him and he said the same thing: She was kind, generous, helpful, and devoted to family.

Margo was overwhelmed when I told her about Joan's tragic life. She hoped that one day she would be able to share this information with her mother.

I got back to Margo and said, "I know a lot about Joan's parents and your mom would be proud of her heritage."

Mary lives only two hours from me. What a joy it would be to meet her!

～

As I was learning about Mary, my half-sister, and trying to help her daughters understand Joan's tragic life, I was drawn back into the search for my birthfather. After all, my adoption story was unfinished--and I knew there were search angels and strategies available to help. ***I also knew the answer was hidden in DNA***. I reached out once again to the Facebook closed group, *DNA Detectives*. If I could learn how to build mirror trees, I might solve the mystery! Mirror trees can be confusing. I defer to the experts for a definition. The online site, *DNAeXplained – Genetic Genealogy*, has the following definition:

> Mirror trees are a technique that genealogists use to help identify a missing common ancestor by recreating the tree of a match and strategically attaching your DNA to their tree to see who you match that descends from which line in their tree.

Phew! Got that?

A wonderfully helpful search angel in *DNA Detectives* offered help, and we got started on my first mirror tree. One of my close matches has a well-developed family tree. We recreated it and matched my DNA to the tree. It was slow difficult work. After a month, our progress was minimal.

My search angel explained that endogamy, or inbreeding, made the search especially difficult. Endogamy was common in the area around the St. Lawrence River and the Maritime provinces. I knew from my AncestryDNA Ethnicity Estimate, that many of my ancestors lived along the St. Lawrence River. Interestingly, I'd always been curious about one surname that appeared on both my maternal and paternal match lists!

I was working many hours every day filling in the family tree to include all family members of a generation, all spouses and children, etc. The bigger the tree, the more chances to identify a common ancestor.

~

Finally, my search angel recommended a genealogist in Montreal, Vanessa Laframboise. *Laframboise Genealogy* is her business, but she also volunteers her time to assist folks like Marc and me. We were thrilled to have Vanessa's help. A professional genealogist! We shared everything we knew with Vanessa: DNA results from all companies, family trees, and family stories!

My favorite exchange came in the middle of the first day she worked on our case, October 25, 2017: "I found out where you connect with other matches. Onésime and Marie Tremblay are your great-grandparents. I don't know if you mind, but would you please give me the permission to build a tree for you?"

Whoa! Of course, I didn't mind. I was thrilled. Vanessa wanted to build a tree without my help! She even asked me kindly not to touch it. This was the best news I'd heard in a long time.

And when I mentioned endogamy, she said it didn't bother her at all. "It doesn't really matter to me. I've never had a problem with it...yet."

Marc and I each had a number of DNA matches in the second to third-cousin range. Vanessa tried to figure out *how* they matched us. Who were our shared ancestors? Nineteenth-century families had many children. It was common to have ten to twelve children.

Adding to the challenge, each child typically had three first names. In French Canada, Catholic family names often began with Joseph for a baby boy or Marie for a baby girl. Traditionally, but not always, the second name was the name of a godfather or godmother. The third name was typically the one used in daily life. And in adulthood, the third name appears on records of marriage or their children's birth and baptisms, or their death certificates. First and second names were dropped over time. This issue became relevant for me, as I'll explain shortly.

In my opinion, the most reliable records were baptismal records. Birth certificates may be missing, but original baptismal records survived and include both parents' names, Godparents, often grandparents, and important dates. I began to rely on baptismal records. Census records and voting lists were also helpful. Marc and I needed to find a family that lived in Verdun from 1948, when I was conceived, to 1959 when he was conceived! I kept finding families in the Quebec City area. I thought I'd never find anyone from Verdun.

We got closer when my search angel in the closed Facebook group, *Free Canada Adoption/Family Search and Reunion*, sent me a message containing new information. Annie Carlile is her name and she has helped me many times over the last few years. Annie is quick and thorough. I don't know how she finds documents I can't find. I am always amazed by her and so appreciative!

Here's her message to me November 26, 2017: "Well, I found a link between a Kelley family connected to one of your matches who married into another Kelly family connected to Onésime Ouellet and Marie Tremblay."

A Kelly married a Kelley! I'm dumbfounded!

And that family was Gerard Kelley, married 21 June 1927 Quebec City to Ida Kelly. And they had a lot of children who married in the Montreal area. They didn't have a son named Ronald Kelly, but they had one named Joseph Gerard René Kelley, b. 1931.

Annie then sent me her typed notes, with the details of my paternal heritage dating all the way back to my great-grand-parents. She connected a couple of my DNA cousin matches, including the numbers of shared chromosomes with shared ancestors! Using that strategy, she had found a family with a number of sons from Verdun! That's why she's called a search *angel!* I didn't ask her to do the research and type up her notes. She simply decided one day to work on my birthfather case! *I thank you forever, Annie. You are an angel!*

I shared Annie's findings with Vanessa. Vanessa then updated my mirror tree. Not only was the name Kelly, but a Kelley married a Kelly! Was Ellen at Batshaw telling the truth after all? She hadn't denied the name Kelly. Vanessa also continued to build out the tree to catch more matches. Our next challenge was to get DNA proof that we had our family.

~

I was having a difficult time finding any information on Joseph Gerard René Kelley. I found only one source—his baptismal record! It stated that René was the name of his Godfather, even though it was the third name. Vanessa referred to him as Joseph Gerard R. Kelley. She was sure he would have been known as Gerard. But from Marc's experience, the name next to the surname is the name used. Accordingly, I thought I'd try and search for René Kelley.

I found a voting record from 1957 for René Kelley, with his wife's name below his. If his godfather was named René, as stated on the baptismal record, I would expect René to be his second name, not the third name. Rules are meant to be broken, right? Joseph Gerard René Kelley went by René Kelley. Was I getting closer?

Vanessa emphasized the need for DNA evidence. I was in total agreement, but I wanted more information from the mirror trees. I wasn't ready to make cold calls, asking for saliva samples. In mid-December, I received a new second-cousin match. Vanessa figured out where he fit in the family tree.

She was quite pleased because it strengthened the probability that René Kelley was my birthfather, "Perhaps you found the right guy. You should contact someone close to this man."

I was delighted! My genealogist and search angel were now on the same page! I *was* getting closer!

Later that day, Vanessa wrote, "I have found Gerard Kelley's obituary. Your grandfather."

Vanessa also sent me notes on both sides of my birthfather's family tree. I filled in details and dates and finally created family trees for both sides of my supposed birthfather's family. I named my work, *Heritage Proposal*. Genealogy is somewhat complicated, and I've tweaked it a number of times. Here is the full title:

Searching for Birthfathers:

Bonnie Parsons and Marc Mercier ~
1st Cousins!
with
Vanessa Laframboise, Genealogist &
Annie Carlile, Search Angel

Heritage Proposal

Soon we had photos of both of René's parents—Marc's and my grandparents. René's obituary followed. He died June 6, 2012. The obituary did not include family names. However, we had enough information to get the names of siblings. Annie had listed nine children in this family from Verdun. Marc and I were thrilled!

~

Marc's career is in information technology. He knows how to find information online, including in Facebook! When he has a good lead, he fearlessly writes, requests "friends," and makes phone calls! One of René's sisters, who is no longer living, had four daughters. Marc found them on Facebook and left messages. They did not respond immediately, which is always a worry because we really wanted and needed their cooperation. When he did hear from them, they were friendly. What a relief! They said he should call their Aunt Kathleen, because she knows details about the family better than anyone.

Aunt Kathleen is indeed incredible. She is known for her amazing memory. She is another angel in my realm. I called her after Marc called her. It was one of those conversations that filled my heart with love and appreciation. I'll never forget it. René was five years older than Kathleen. I started to tell her Joan's name, and she interrupted me:

Joan Williamson? I remember Joan Williamson. I remember when she and René were dating. They dated for five or six months. Joan would come over to our house and visit with our mother until René got home from work. She would often bring something sweet, cookies or candy. Mom and Joan got along really well. Mom loved Joan! Joan was really beautiful, light hair, about 5'4". Then suddenly she stopped coming around. I asked my mom where Joan is, and she didn't know, only that she doesn't come around anymore.

I was scribbling notes as fast as I could when I realized I was more interested in this information about Joan than finding out about René. I was taken by surprise and thrilled to hear nice things about Joan. Kathleen told me their street address back then. I looked it up, and they were about a half mile from Joan's house on Wellington Street. I could picture Joan

243

walking happily to René's when she got home from work, carrying a treat for his mother. I was also thrilled to learn how my life began. Joan and René were in love, *young love!*

Kathleen is sure René did not know Joan was pregnant, or that she gave birth to a baby girl and named her Betty. Kathleen said that, had their father known about the pregnancy, he would have wanted to keep me. He would never have agreed to adoption. A few years later, René got married had two sons. I was his only daughter.

Kathleen had more to tell me—she and her husband had moved their family down to Hemmingford back in the 1970s. They wanted their children to experience living in the country. They were there for eight years. I was stunned when she told me that they lived directly across the street from Johnnie Walker, and they saw Joan every weekend when she came down from Verdun. Holy cow, so much information! One day, Kathleen's mother came down to visit. Joan was at Johnnie's. Kathleen's mother, Ida, and Joan were so happy to see each other. Kathleen described Joan as "lively and friendly, self-assured, always well-dressed, and her hair was beautiful."

After Kathleen and I spoke, she talked to her three adult children. She asked if they remembered Joan Williamson. Each one had fond memories of Joan in Hemmingford.

A couple of years later, it was Johnnie Walker who told Kathleen, "Joan passed away." Kathleen attended Joan's funeral in July 1983. Her personal knowledge of Joan was shocking and thrilling at the same time.

~

I remember the first time I spoke to Joan's brother, back in 1988. I felt overwhelmed that I was talking to someone who knew my birthmother. Now thirty years later, I felt the same way talking to Kathleen. She is a link between Joan and me.

She is also a link between René and me. No one else that I know of knew both Joan and René as well as Kathleen did. When she looks at me in photos or when we FaceTime, she recognizes both Joan and René in me.

I felt like celebrating! There was no celebrating the day I was born, but I could now celebrate knowing the identity of my birthparents and hearing everything Kathleen shared with me.

René had his own upholstery business, now owned by one of his sons. In Chapter 5, I wrote about my first sewing lesson. My mom was my clever mentor! Now I know that sewing was important on both sides of my family. I also love to play the piano. Joan's father played the church organ every Sunday and Kathleen told me that her dad played piano! Both of my grandfathers played the piano. It is a joy to find out about my blood relatives, my families of origin!

Kathleen really wanted the two of us to chat on FaceTime. But, I hesitated--I needed the DNA evidence that René was my birthfather before I could feel comfortable on FaceTime. Everything Kathleen remembered about Joan and René was wonderful. However, I'd been in this situation before with Joanne! This time had to be different. I needed to get DNA proof.

~

I knew the best choices for a high match were with René's two sons. If I matched with either one of them, I would have the DNA proof that René was my birthfather. René's older son, Yves, agreed to help me out! I ordered the AncestryDNA kit, downloaded the French-language instructions for him, and mailed it FedEx International Priority to Montreal. The rules had changed since I registered Lillian's kit from my computer. They now required Yves to register his own kit. An added challenge for all of us was that both of René's sons and their families speak primarily French. Yves's wife, Lucie, helped out—she is more comfortable with English. Lucie let me know when the kit arrived, and when it was mailed back to AncestryDNA. I estimated we would not get the results until mid-March. I restrained myself from being overly confident while I waited to hear from Yves and Lucie.

～

But then on March seventh, at 5:52 a.m., I got a text message from Marc: "**I have a new cousin, Yves Kelly, hope it says brother for you!!!**"

The results are in! I grabbed my laptop. Finally, the proof! And there he was! Category, "Close Family," right under Mary, my maternal half-sister. Yves and I share 1647 cM and 51 DNA segments!

I sent screenshots of the results to Vanessa Laframboise and Annie Carlile for verification, and they both agreed: "Yves is your half-brother!" René is his father **and** my father.

The thirty-five-year search is over. I have DNA proof!

Marc translated my note to French for Yves: "Thank you very much for agreeing to be tested. It means the world to me. Bonnie"

Lucie wrote a message for me from Yves—Marc translated it, "Can you tell Bonnie that Yves has shed a few tears because he is glad that Bonnie can finally make peace with her research. He feels good and happy. He is not a big talker, but he is very touched." And I was very overwhelmed!

～

Not only is my search over, but René's family welcomed us. Kathleen's daughter thanked *me* for searching! I called René's younger son, Gerry, and told him the results. I think he understood my English! He was very happy. He has a sister!

Then I called Kathleen, and we were both so excited. She has now shared the news with many family members. I've messaged with a number of them. One of Gerry's daughters wrote to me recently—a newfound niece! I told Kathleen we would visit Montreal this summer or fall. She was already making plans, just like Joan's brother John did for us in 1988. Kathleen's nieces cautioned her to keep the reunion small at first, so that I wouldn't run away. Don't worry. Not a chance after all this time and effort! Kathleen's husband has old videos that show a young René. He promised to find them for me!

Marc and I are still hoping to solve the question of his birthfather. He is trying to reach a supposed half-brother who might agree to DNA testing. We are quite sure which of René's brothers is his birthfather, but we want DNA proof! His cousin match in AncestryDNA with Yves is a solid piece of the puzzle.

~

When Vanessa agreed to help Marc and me, we knew we would not be paying clients. She wanted to volunteer her assistance because she likes to help others as much as she can. I communicated often with Vanessa. I was always hoping for progress and asking for updates.

She reminded me a couple of times that I wasn't a paying client, to which I replied, "I want to be a paying client!"

Vanessa said it was too late for that--she hadn't been recording the time she spent with me. That's when I decided to make a donation to *Laframboise Genealogy*. And then we were both happy!

I knew that Annie's online group was not a business. But I wanted to do something to express my gratitude. I offered a donation to help out with office supplies, etc.

"What office?" replied Annie.

"I want to make a donation in appreciation for all your help identifying my birthfather," I explained.

Annie said that, in similar situations, people purchased a DNA kit for someone who can't afford one. Later that day, Annie had a name for me. I chose to purchase a FamilyTreeDNA kit in honor of my match with Marc. Our first match was in FamilyTreeDNA!

BIRTHMOTHER: JOAN WILLIAMSON

BIRTHFATHER: RENÉ KELLEY

In June 2018, I applied to the Province of Quebec, under its new law, requesting the name of my birthfather in my adoption file. They verified that his name is in my file, and now I am waiting. Is my birthfather's first name written clearly? And is his last name spelled Kelly or Kelley? I am hoping to learn why Batshaw sent me the details from Ronald Kelly's obituary, stating they believed he was my birthfather.

22

MONTREAL REUNIONS

I always dreamed of returning to Montreal. For thirty-five years, I searched for my biological identity. Whose DNA did I inherit? What were their names, their characteristics and personalities, their abilities, challenges, *and* medical histories? I wanted to receive photos and to meet them, as intimidating as this sounded to me.

In 1988, I went to Montreal for the first time as an adult, to meet my birthmother's family. She had died too young, five years earlier, at age 54. Strangely, I had not been shocked to receive the news of her death from the adoption agency. As she lay dying in a Montreal hospital, I was at home becoming more and more agitated—thinking only about her and finding her. In an eerie way, I did find my birthmother in 1988, when we visited her in the Mount Royal Cemetery.

After our reunion, I moved on by staying in touch with her family. We developed wonderful loving relationships. I always marveled at the fact that my children had a great-grandmother into their teens.

Thirty years later, would the dream to return come true? On March 7, 2018, the DNA results arrived proving Yves and I are half-siblings! René Kelley was my birthfather! Now I knew my dream would come true. I would return to Montreal.

Marc and I had planned on going to Montreal together and celebrating the newfound identities of our birthfathers. We were quite sure which of René's brothers was Marc's birthfather, but we wanted to have the DNA results. Reaching out to people who never knew you existed is a delicate process that can't be rushed.

In addition, I wanted to get to know folks in René's family before we visited them. I communicated through Facebook messaging and FaceTime. It was thrilling! I was elated with each new message.

Marc was also getting to know our new relatives. Ottawa is only a couple of hours from Montreal, and so Marc was able to visit Montreal before I could. We believe the DNA to prove his birthfather's identity will come eventually. Once again, we have to be patient. Gradually, the plan for Montreal came into focus, and we decided to make the trip the last weekend in August.

~

I mapped out Paul's and my itinerary for Friday, Saturday, and Sunday. We approached Montreal from the west on the 401 and stopped in Saint-Lazare to visit with Joan's sister, Doreen—we hadn't seen each other in over twenty years! I always knew I wanted to visit Doreen on the way because it had been so long. We shared photos and chatted about Joan. Doreen showed me a photo album that had belonged to Joan and invited me to take the photos I particularly liked.

I sensed Doreen's conflicting feelings about her older sister. On the one hand, Doreen loved Joan and appreciated all of her best qualities. However, I felt her frustration. Joan gave birth to four babies out of wedlock. She never married.

Doreen knew that their parents lived with this shame for the rest of their lives.

Grandma said, "Joan always kept to herself." I can't help but wonder if communication between Joan and her parents might have helped everyone.

~

After our visit with Doreen, we drove to Sainte-Anne-de-Bellevue, my hometown. Sainte-Anne-de-Bellevue is an on-island suburb at the western tip of Montreal. Our plan was to meet Joanne, Ronald Kelly's daughter. Two years before, Joanne had agreed to DNA testing. I described in Chapter 20 how Joanne and I developed a wonderful friendship during the process of waiting for her DNA kit and then waiting for the results. When the results proved that we were not related, we vowed nevertheless to meet someday and celebrate our *sisterhood*.

We met on Sainte-Anne Street, downtown on the waterfront. Joanne brought her two teenage children. We were so excited! We felt like sisters and found ourselves once again wanting to deny the DNA results. Her kids were delightful. Jasmine and my Emily had kept up with their mothers' friendship. They were particularly excited for us to meet. Jasmine attends Macdonald College, now John Abbott College, and is very familiar with my hometown! We all agreed to keep in touch.

Meeting with Joanne was our first experience with bilingualism during our trip. Joanne and her children are fluent in French and English. It is second nature for them to switch back and forth between the two languages. I recall Joanne telling me how she always wanted her son and daughter to learn both languages when they were young.

For the next two days, we were with folks who were bilingual, as well as many who spoke only French. On a couple of occasions, we were lucky to be with people who understood us! Marc grew up in a French-speaking home. Without a doubt, I am fortunate that he is bilingual. The search for our birthfathers would have been *even more* difficult if he didn't speak English!

~

Saturday was life-changing. I met both of René's sons! They are the closest biological relatives I've met since Joan visited me in foster care when I was an infant. When we left our house Thursday, I wasn't sure if I would be able to meet Gerry. Then, on Friday, his daughter, Jennifer, sent me a text message saying that her father wanted us to come to his house Saturday at 11:00!

We drove from our hotel near Sainte-Anne-de-Bellevue to Chateauguay, south of Montreal, where Gerry and his wife, Lyne, live and where he has his upholstery business. We passed through Kahnawake Mohawk Territory. Paul has studied the history of the Kahnawake and was particularly excited to see the area.

We received a wonderfully warm welcome from Gerry and Lyne. Jennifer was also there with her 7-year-old daughter. Gerry and I were in disbelief! We hugged and kissed and kept looking at each other. I had photos and a couple of gifts from Buffalo, including chicken-wing sauce from Anchor Bar, where chicken wings were invented and became famous! At the same time, they had a gift for me and photos! We were already feeling like family!

Gerry is very adventurous and creative in his work and at home. Each room is artfully decorated. René loved to play pool, and now Gerry honors the family tradition with a cleverly designed poolroom! In another room, he has a display of family photos. As we were enjoying the photos, Gerry told us that his dad said, on more than one occasion, "I always wanted a daughter." *Wow!* We all wondered if René knew about me or had an awareness on a spiritual level. It was one of the most memorable moments of our trip.

Before heading to Yves's house, we met Marc at the motel to check in. Marc was just arriving from Ottawa. In this rural area, everyone speaks French and has little need to speak English. In more urban communities, business folks are bilingual so that they can do business with all their customers. But in this motel—not so much! Thank you, Marc, for checking us in!

Next, the three of us drove to Yves and Lucie's house in St-Michel. The GPS on my cell phone got us there—in fact, it was a godsend the entire trip!

Yves and Lucie had been planning their party for us since the DNA results came back positive in March. They'd waited for me to set a date and been prepared months in advance of our arrival! All their kids and grandkids were there. Yves came out to the car and met us. He and I were in disbelief, as Gerry and I had been. Yves speaks a little English, and I speak even less French. We did our best. Others chimed in to help and Marc was there.

Lucie planned everything: backyard games, snacks, dinner, and a campfire. They had photos for me, and I shared mine and gave them gifts from Buffalo. The photos showed our resemblances, but the stunner was being there with Yves's son and daughter, who look so much like Ron and Emily, and a granddaughter who looks like the twin of one of our granddaughters. Paul and I couldn't believe our eyes!

Yves's son loves baseball. His daughter plays baseball and softball. Baseball is the number one sport for Ron and our grandson! Both of Ron and Kim's daughters play softball.

All three families love cats. Yves introduced us to his Maine Coon. Gerry's daughter, Jennifer, has three cats, and Emily has two Ragdoll kitties. Paul and I had five cats over the years.

Saturday was a day like no other! I believe it was the beginning of new friendships—with family connections we never knew we had. They welcomed me, and I am forever grateful for their generous hospitality and kindness.

~

On Sunday, we were heading back into Montreal, to the borough of LaSalle, to meet Aunt Kathleen and her family. With my cell phone GPS to guide us, we took the lead and Marc followed in his car. Kathleen and Roger greeted us with another warm welcome! Their daughter, Lisa, was there, too. Kathleen had been excited from the very first moment she learned about Marc and me. I knew her better than I knew Gerry and Yves because we had talked and seen each other on FaceTime prior to our trip.

We had a wonderful visit sharing photos and learning who was who in Kathleen's photos from years ago. It was fun to see how much I look like my birthfather, René. Kathleen says that, when she looks at me now, she sees her brother. My laugh always reminds her of René!

Roger had the home videos ready to show us. I always wanted to see what my birthfather looked like as a young man, and this was my opportunity. What a treat! I am so grateful to Roger for retrieving the videos from their basement and having them ready for us.

We topped off our visit with lunch at Bocci Resto-Café in LaSalle. Lisa's husband joined us. Everything was delightful!

It was difficult to say goodbye. I knew our trip was coming to a close.

BOCCI RESTO-CAFÉ IN LASALLE. BACK ROW: BONNIE, PAUL, KATHLEEN, AND ALAIN. FRONT ROW: LISA, MARC, AND ROGER

I love the way Marc and I keep up with texts and long, delightful phone calls. Now I will try to do the same with Gerry, Yves, Kathleen, and their families. Paul and I look forward to visiting Montreal more often. It's important for all of us to keep the dream alive.

Joanne and I will always be close. We know that DNA does not tell the whole story in friendship and love.

~

After our goodbyes, we went back to Baie-D'Urfé to the same hotel we'd stayed at Friday night. The next morning, we returned to Sainte-Anne-de-Bellevue. I desperately wanted to visit my early memories and take some photos. I found I was able to navigate the quaint little streets without my GPS! However, I couldn't believe how much my hometown appeared to have shrunk! The streets never used to look so little and the houses so close together. I was sure the home economics building was way down the street, but it's next door!

I took photos of Glenaladale Terrace—our home when I was first adopted. I also got a shot of the Maple Avenue house.

We stopped at the school where, in kindergarten, I decided I wanted to be a teacher. My grade 2 class photo was taken at the front entrance. I am in the middle of the front row. A photo of that entrance today shows the same concrete pillars from the 1950s.

ELEMENTARY SIDE OF MACDONALD HIGH SCHOOL

SCHOOL FRONT DOORS TODAY

GRADE 2 CLASS PHOTO - 1956

Eventually, I felt ready to move on and we left Sainte-Anne-de-Bellevue for home.

MY BELOVED GINKGO TREE IS STILL THERE, LOOMING LARGE NOW!

MAPLE AVENUE HOME

~

I had a lot to do and process when the trip was over. I wanted to express my gratitude to Yves, Gerry, and Kathleen and their families for welcoming us into their homes. The next day, I sent thank you bouquets and notes. I text messaged with Jennifer, Lucie, and Lisa. Gerry's wife, Lyne, called to thank me for the flowers. Lyne speaks very little English. When we were in their home on Saturday, Jennifer translated everything for her. I was truly touched by Lyne's thoughtfulness. I knew it wasn't easy for her. Kathleen and I have FaceTimed a couple of times since our trip. We will always be here for each other!

In closing, I feel a great sense of relief and joy. With help and support from search angels, friends, and my family, *I know the identity of my birthparents.*

My newfound awareness of the needs of birthmothers enabled me to understand Joan's decisions to relinquish four infants. She had brought tremendous shame to her family and lacked the support to care for her babies.

I have also learned and grown in my understanding of adoption issues. Babies have rights too! Identity is sacred. Original birth certificates should never be altered or replaced. Upon adoption, a new certificate is necessary, but it shouldn't state that another woman gave birth to the child. Babies have the right to know about their biological heritage--they have the right to inquire about their birthparents and obtain their hospital record of birth. Finally, adoptees and birthparents should be able to find one another and be reunited if they choose.

These issues are often delicate and difficult. We need support in our decision-making, and most importantly, we need adoption laws on our side. Thank you to all the advocates for change who work tirelessly for the rights of adoptees and parents! In the future, with updated laws, DNA, and social media, answers should be accessible in a more reasonable timeframe.

EPILOGUE

May 2019: After a yearlong wait, the Province of Quebec finally gave me the name of my birthfather as it appears in my adoption file. Batshaw thought my birthfather was Ronald Kelly and gave me the details of his death from the Montreal Gazette. The details were considered non-identifying information. However, they were substantial enough for me to find his name in the Gazette obituaries. Ronald Kelly's youngest daughter is Joanne Kelly. She kindly and generously agreed to have her DNA tested. We both wanted proof that Ronald Kelly was my birthfather and that we were half-sisters! We waited patiently for the results, cautiously confident. When they arrived, we were shocked to see that Joanne's DNA did not match my DNA. We were also completely baffled—why did Batshaw give me the details for Ronald Kelly? He is not my birthfather.

DNA has since proven that René Kelley was my birthfather. The misunderstanding occurred back in 1948 when Joan was pregnant with me. The cause of the misunderstanding was the pronunciation of René's name. René's family pronounces René: Ree'-nee. Joan and the adoption caseworker both spoke English. René's family also spoke English but used the French pronunciation of his name.

Joan didn't write her answers in the interview—they were typed by the Ville Marie interviewer who thought Joan said Ronnie when she actually said Ree'-nee for René. Thus, the file says my birthfather's name was *Ronnie Kelly*! I relayed this information to Joanne immediately. She said that, in French, they do sound similar. I also learned that her father grew up in Rosemont, about ten miles from Joan's and René's families in Verdun. René's younger sister, Kathleen, remembers when Joan and René were dating.

The Batshaw caseworker who called me was extremely kind and helpful. She actually took the time to read my file before she called to give me my birthfather's name, as it appeared in my file. She made sure I understood that Joan did not write the answers—they were typed by the interviewer. I have spoken to many Batshaw adoption caseworkers during the last 36 years—this one is an angel to me! In the end, I needed more than the DNA match to solve the mystery of Ronnie and René. Thankfully, my search angel reread my file and figured it out. She is fluent in French and English and knows the different pronunciations of René. *Finally, the mystery was solved!*

～

My newest search angel had one more thing to tell me. Eight months earlier, I was told that a sibling wanted to meet me! I hoped it was Joan's youngest child. I promptly submitted the forms and had been waiting all these months. Now Batshaw was finally ready to give my half-sibling and me permission to communicate. My search angel said that, having read my file, she knew I did not like the Batshaw rules regarding monitored letter exchanges. She agreed that since my half-sibling and I wanted to exchange emails, we should just go ahead. Some rules are indeed meant to be broken. And yes, my half-sibling is Joan's youngest—47 years old, beautiful and smart, and fluent in English, French, and Spanish!

My Batshaw search angel has seen me to the end of the line. I've learned the identity of my birthparents and half-siblings—three from Joan and two from René. I appreciate her thoughtful feedback, "Your persistence was incredible and having reunited with your siblings, supporting them as well, is truly a hallmark of what older siblings do." She explained to me that her career was winding down and she would be retiring at the end of the month!

At her request, I was pleased to share my blog, particularly the Mother's Day post: https://younglove-anadopteesmemoir.com/2019/05/08/sunday-is-mothers-day.

Finally, I was thrilled to read: *"I want to thank you for sharing your blog. Part of you stays with us now as your Mother's Day post will be used for sensitization training for future adoptive parents."*

ACKNOWLEDGMENTS

I searched for my birthparents for thirty-five years. During the last six years, I have worked on this memoir. My husband, Paul, and children, Ron and Emily, have been unwavering in their understanding and support. They never questioned nor complained about my need to find answers to my identity. Their unconditional love enabled me to complete my search and tell my story.

Thank you, Mom and Dad, for your love and support. When I wanted to begin my search, you immediately helped me contact the adoption agency. In many ways, this memoir is a tribute to both of you along with my love and appreciation.

My Grandpa Crawford had many hobbies. Photography was a favorite. Several of his photos are included in this memoir. I especially appreciate the cover shot of me with my beautiful sailboat, a treasured gift from Grandpa and Nana.

Difficult tasks in life are much easier to endure with support and friendship. Marc Mercier and I worked together as soon as we learned about our 1st cousin DNA match. I am forever grateful to Marc for his humor, technology skills, and bilingual ability. Thank you, Marc, for always adding fun to our search!

DNA testing is at the heart of family searches today. Finding *no match* can be as important as finding a match! I am also forever grateful to Joanne Kelly and Yves Kelly for agreeing to submit AncestryDNA test kits on my behalf. The results brought closure to my search after all these years.

AncestryDNA has identified one of my half-sisters and most recently another half-brother. In both cases, their daughters have written to me. I appreciate their curiosity and their willingness to introduce themselves. Hopefully, with encouragement from their families, my siblings and I will meet some day.

I couldn't have searched for my birth family and written this story without the support of many search angels along the way. Candy and Bev at *Parent Finders Montreal* were my first mentors in the search process. Vicki Hunt has helped me since 2014—always upbeat, faithful, and quick to respond! Members and administrators in Facebook's *DNA Detectives,* and its subgroup *DD Social,* are ready 24/7 to guide, inform, refer, and encourage. A sweet angel from Louisiana picked up my case and got me started with mirror trees. Marie from *The ALMA Society* steered me to request that the adoption agency inform my maternal half-siblings of their medical history. Annie Carlile from Facebook's *Free Canada Adoption/Family Search and Reunion* has provided documents and data for me for years, particularly this past year. Heartfelt gratitude to search angels everywhere!

Lorraine Dusky, friend and author of *hole in my heart,* helped me understand the tragedy birthmothers experience when they relinquish a baby. Lorraine's blog, *[birthmother] First Mother Forum,* is informative and always enlightening.

Liz Langland and I are dear friends from high school. She knew my parents and brother and sister. Liz is an author and historian. While I have been writing this memoir, Liz has helped me make significant content decisions. And she always makes me feel like I am doing the right thing!

Lucy Miskin, retired publisher from Acton, Massachusetts, provided encouragement and information on publishing. She was also a friend and supporter of my elderly mother-in-law in Acton when we couldn't be there.

I read and love Dianne Riordan's memoir, *The Names of My Mothers*. Dianne lives in Buffalo and agreed to meet with me. She gave me helpful advice on writing, editing, and publishing. Mostly, I appreciate Dianne's kind and encouraging words.

Kathleen, Roger, Lisa, Yves, Lucie, Gerry, Lyne, Jennifer, and families, thank you for welcoming Paul and me into your homes for our Montreal reunion, August 2018! Our gratitude extends beyond words for your love and hospitality. We will keep the Montreal dream alive!

Ellie Woznica designed the cover and the text of my memoir. I am very grateful for her creativity and hard work. Sarah McMichael helped edit with a fine eye for detail. I have never met anyone who loves punctuation as much as Sarah!

London Metropolitan Archives stores the London Foundling Hospital records. I feel so fortunate to have received copies of the original 1870 petition by my twice great-grandmother to have her son admitted to the LFH. These are treasured documents!

~

Dear Joan,

Thank you for communicating to Rose at Lily Dale. Rose explained to me that the spirits of our strongest loves come through to her. I am so grateful. I believe you are with me, and I hope we meet again.

Love, Bonnie

Dear René,

I am the daughter you wished for. I am sorry we missed the opportunity to meet one another. But I am getting to know you through your family, and I believe we would have had a wonderful reunion and times together! After all, we have the same smile.

Love, Bonnie

HELPFUL RESOURCES

It is often as simple as knowing where to look. The following resources were helpful to me during my search. By including them, I hope to help other searchers find answers that lead them closer to reunions with their birth families!

1. **Child Welfare Information Gateway**
   Link: https://www.childwelfare.gov/topics/system-wide/laws-policies/statutes/infoaccessap
   Phone: 1-800-394-3366

2. **Batshaw Youth and Family Centres**
   Link: http://www.batshaw.qc.ca/en
   Phone: 514-989-1885

3. **ALMA—Adoptees' Liberty Movement Association (ALMA)**
   Link: http://almasociety.org/

4. **[birthmother] First Mother Forum**
   Authors: Lorraine Dusky and Jane Edwards)
   Link: https://www.firstmotherforum.com/

5. **Birthmark (1979)**
   Author: Lorraine Dusky

6. **hole in my heart (2015)**
   Author: Lorraine Dusky

7. **Facebook DNA Detectives**
   Link: https://www.facebook.com/TheDNADetectives/

8. **Facebook Free Canada Adoption / Family Search and Reunion**
   Link: https://www.facebook.com/groups/CanadaAdoptees

9. **Family Tree DNA**
   Link: https://www.familytreedna.com/

10. **Ancestry**
    Link: ancestry.com

11. **London Metropolitan Archives (Paid Document Research Service)**
    Link: https://wwwcityoflondon.govuk/things-to-do/london-metropolitana

12. **Findmypast**
    Link: findmypast.com

13. **DNAeXplained – Genetic Genealogy**
    Link: https://dna-explained.com/

14. **Laframboise Genealogy**
    Author: Vanessa Laframboise
    Link: https://www.facebook.com/VLGenealogy

15. **Parent Finders of Canada**
    Link: https://parentfindersottawa.ca/

16. **Parent Finders (United States)**
    Link: https://www.parentfinder.com/

17. **My WordPress Blog**
    Link: https://younglove-anadopteesmemoir.com/

Printed in Canada